While I Was Waiting on God, He Was Waiting on Me

A REAL-WORLD GUIDE TO PATIENCE, PURPOSE, AND PERSONAL GROWTH

JONVOANA R. EVANS

First Printing, 2025

Hardback ISBN: 979-8-9878558-8-1

Paperback ISBN:979-8-9878558-9-8

E-Book ISBN: 979-8-9878558-7-4

Printed in the United States of America

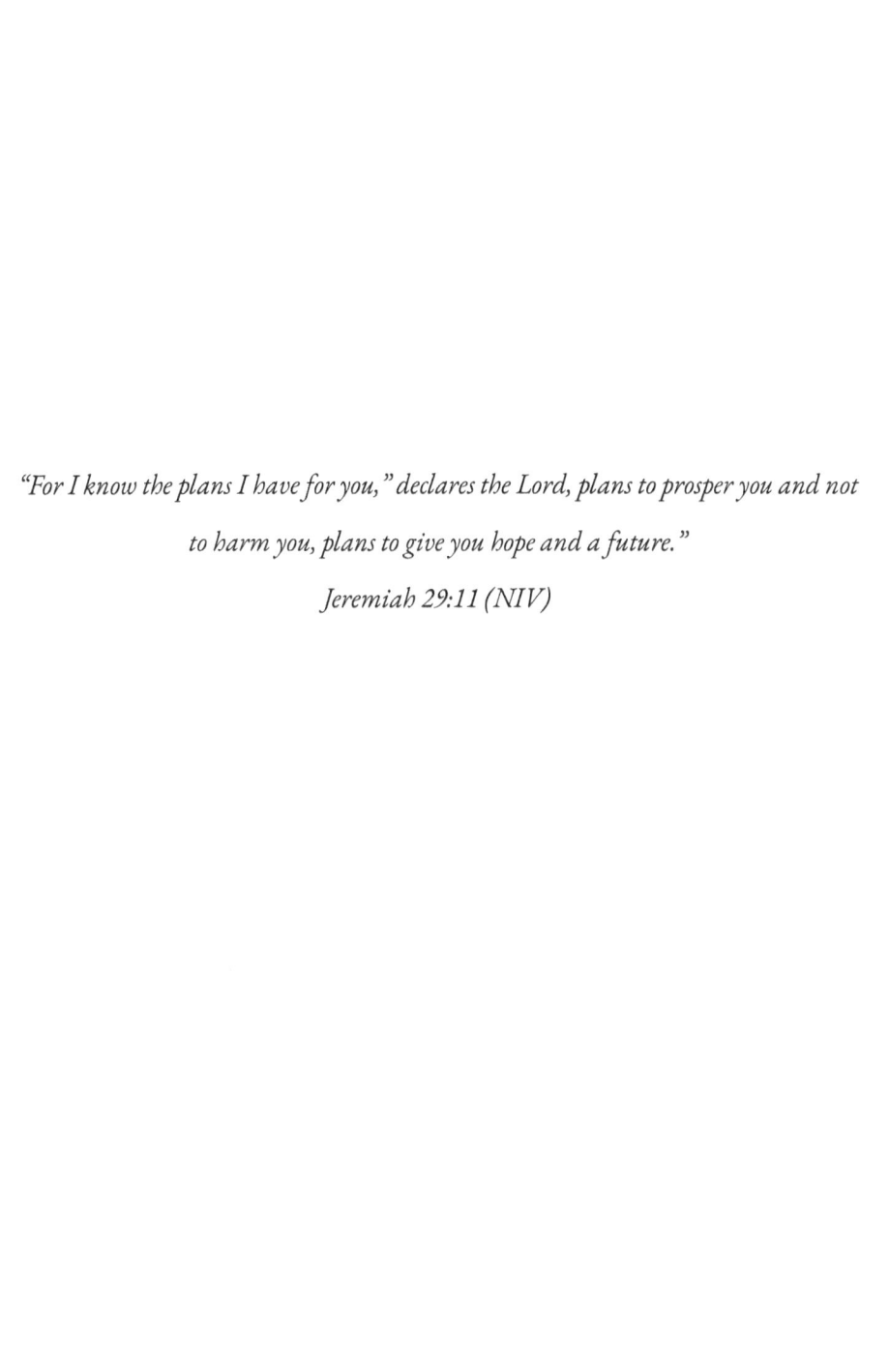

"For I know the plans I have for you," declares the Lord, plans to prosper you and not to harm you, plans to give you hope and a future."

Jeremiah 29:11 (NIV)

Contents

Dedication   VII

Acknowledgements   IX

In Loving Memory   XIII

A Butterfly's Transformation   1

Introduction   3

Chapter 1 Waiting Is Inevitable   9

Chapter 2 Two Perspectives   17

Chapter 3 Butterfly Obsession   25

The Butterfly Life Cycle: The Stages of Waiting   31

Chapter 4 The Egg Stage   33

Chapter 5 Stage 2: The Caterpillar Stage   65

Chapter 6 The Chrysalis Stage   117

Chapter 7 The Emergence Stage   173

Chapter 8 The Adult Butterfly Stage   219

Chapter 9 The Rebirth   261

Chapter 10 The Cycle   275

Special Note to Aspiring Life Coaches and World Changers   291

The Cycle Resources Guide   293

   Stages of the Butterfly Life Cycle: Quick Reference Guide   297

   A Butterfly's Prayer of Surrender   301

   Patience in Practice   303

   Grounded in Gratitude   309

   While They Waited: Lessons in Patience from the Bible   313

   Affirming the Cycle   319

   The Butterfly Atrium Creed   323

About the Author   327

Dedication

This book is dedicated to my king, my husband, my very best friend, and my best part, the priest of our household. Thank you for being the epitome of what it means to love someone. Your unwavering consistency has been the most life-changing presence in my life on erff, and I know with everything in me that God gifted you to me. Thank you for showing me what commitment between a husband and wife is, the meaning of support between friends, and the strength of partnership between two individuals from two different sides of the railroad tracks.

When you asked me to take this scroll with you, and I said yes, it became a beautiful dance. Even with a few stepping on of toes and, at times, moving to a different beat, you never let go of my hand. You chose to stand by me during some of the toughest times, and you never made it feel like an obligation. Not only did you stay with me, but you also prayed with me, encouraged me, and led me. What we have is BEAMAZING. King, I see the divine in you!

T&B, ~ Queen

Acknowledgements

God... All Glory Belongs to You!

To my daughters, the 3T's, thank you for forgiving me and loving me despite my cluelessness in figuring out motherhood. You three have shared some of the hardest times of my personal growth, often bearing the brunt of the lessons I had to learn. I am so proud, blessed, and honored that God chose me to be called Mom by you. I love you all deeply and pray that I continue to make you proud to call me Mom. Thank you for cheering me on and holding me accountable while navigating this unknown territory.

To my bonus babies, the 2 Rs, thank you for proving that family is more than just blood relations. You have added a new dimension of love to my life.

To my Granny, Delores Shipley, I pray that your eyes can read, your ears can hear, and your heart can feel all the love and intention that comes from these pages. Over the past 10 years, since the day I met you, you have been such an instrumental part of my life. Thank you for your unconditional love and prayers. I love you.

To my parents, Darlene & Levern, parents-in-love, grandparents, my family, friends, and all those who have supported, prayed for, encouraged, loved, guided, lovingly corrected, embraced, and trusted me through my process.

To two very special accountability partners who shared this journey with me, like it was their own—while I attempted to keep it a surprise for my husband, Nikki Carol and Althea. Thank you both so much for delighting in my vision, praying for and with me, crying with me, making the time and taking the initiative to check on me, and helping me navigate challenges. I honestly don't know what this process would've been like without you both!

To my book coach, Dr. Pamela Gurley. Your guidance and expertise, your challenging words, and your celebrations have unlocked and sparked something hidden and untapped. Thank you for all that you've done. I am extremely grateful!

To Oprah. Yes, THE Oprah. Thank you. God had commissioned me to start writing this book without a title and assured me that it would be revealed later. As a natural engineer, this approach was very unorthodox for me, as starting with structure and a foundation is essential. It was like planning to call it a house without having any walls or boundaries.

I was in the gym on November 30, 2023, at 9:15 am, much later than usual, listening to one of your audiobooks when an overwhelming feeling hit me like a ton of bricks, followed by butterflies in my stomach. God had made it clear! I literally wanted to run around the gym screaming. After ensuring it wasn't taken, it was on and poppin' from there! Thank you for unlocking the title of such an intimate part of me, for it is more than just a name—it is the essence of my journey, a reflection of my heart, and a beacon for others to find their way.

To my biggest cheerleaders, Nisha & Lisa, y'all already know! To the queens of YANA FLY, thank you for being the first group to allow me to provide you all with support and guidance, even while navigating through all of my stages. The journey we took together was uncertain. However, what was certain was our forever bond and sisterhood. I am so blessed to have been a part of your lives!

In Loving Memory

To those who have played an integral part in me living out my purpose and personal growth. Your impact lives on in every life that I touch.

Warleshia Wells

LaVersa Campbell

Julie & Reginald Washington

To the Reader,

As you journey through this book, I'm offering you a glimpse into the many layers of who I am—the poetic and playful, the intelligent and idiot, the confident and the cautious, the righteous and ratchet. It's all here, unapologetically me.

My hope is that as you turn these pages, you'll not only find inspiration but also discover the courage to pursue your goals and dreams with intention. May this book encourage you to live more authentically, your unique self, with grace, compassion, and a little less judgment.

Here's to finding patience, purpose, and freedom in every stage of your journey.

~ Jonvoana

A Butterfly's Transformation

"Von is a powerhouse life coach. From the first session to the last, Coach Von never failed to provide perspective, insight, and information that truly added value to my life and circumstances. She is authentic, approachable, patient, kind, understanding, compassionate, and empathetic, with a high mental and emotional IQ. She created a space where I could bring the most vulnerable, unabashed version of myself to every session. With Coach Von's guidance, I grew in meaningful ways over the past six months.

Prior to our sessions, I had not traveled in over 15 years. Under her tutelage, I've traveled twice in the past two months and have two cruises planned by the end of the year. She helped me reduce my anxiety, focus on tasks within my control, and prepare mentally and emotionally to navigate the unfamiliar in a healthy way. Von also coached me to relax, trust the process, and be okay with the "unknown" aspects of life. She showed me how to break the process into small, achievable, and intentional steps. Because of her guidance, planning vacations and stepping into new environments became far less overwhelming. I experienced less fear, less anxiety, and more mental and emotional clarity. Essentially, Coach Von provided me with the tools to have sustainably active confidence. She worked with me to expect the unknown, breathe through it, and remain flexible in unfamiliar situations.

In short, Von helped me become a greatly improved, more certain version of myself. This transformation wasn't just about probing the concept of confidence; it was about exploring who I am and my capabilities. Her work empowered me to take those tiny but incredibly necessary first steps in that journey and embrace all the tears, joy, encouragement, connections, and blessings that unfolded from that lotus flower thereafter."

~ C. Stanley

As you journey through this book, you'll encounter more stories, shared in their own words, and I promise, no bribes were involved (wink) of transformations like this. These testimonies are just some of the many that are here to remind you that you are not alone in this process. Let them inspire and motivate you to keep turning the pages and embrace your own metamorphosis.

Introduction

Stories like the one you've just read remind us of the incredible power of patience and perseverance. But let's be honest—one of the hardest things for us to do is wait. And waiting patiently? That's often out of the question. Why? Because we often associate waiting with inconvenience, as if our time is more important than anyone else's. Don't agree?

Well, let me remind you of what waiting patiently means. It's enduring a period of delay or inactivity without griping, complaining, being annoyed, becoming frustrated, anxious, or upset. It involves maintaining a calm and composed attitude, trusting that the desired outcome or event will occur in due time. This mindset embraces acceptance of the current moment and a willingness to let events unfold naturally without trying to rush or force them. Now, do we agree? Good!

If you or someone you know finds it difficult to wait patiently, read on to discover what impatience does to us mentally, physically, and spiritually. Learn how to navigate the waiting game more graciously, thus improving your overall quality of life. You'll be amazed how learning this simple shift in perspective can transform your experiences and bring a sense of peace to your everyday life.

Interestingly, we frequently find ourselves in situations where waiting feels inevitable. But here's the truth: some waits are completely out of our control, while others are influenced by choices we've made—or failed to make. Understanding the difference can help us approach waiting with greater clarity and intention.

For example, think about waiting in traffic. While we can't control the congestion on the roads, we can adjust our expectations and plan ahead. Setting the goal of arriving early, rather than aiming for a 'just in time' arrival, can alleviate the frustration that comes with unexpected delays. Or consider the long lines at the grocery store. While we can't control how many people decide to shop at the same time, we can choose to shop during off-peak hours or plan ahead, so we don't wait until the last minute to restock.

These small adjustments may not eliminate waiting altogether, but they can reduce unnecessary delays caused by procrastination or poor planning. When we take ownership of the things we can influence, we free up mental and emotional energy to better cope with the waits we can't control.

By distinguishing between what's within our power and what isn't, we set ourselves up for a more peaceful waiting experience. And for those situations where waiting truly is inevitable? That's where patience becomes not just a virtue but a necessity—a skill we can cultivate to navigate life's uncertainties with grace.

"Coach, I thought you were supposed to be helping me navigate the waiting game, not making me feel worse about it!" You're absolutely right—but I wanted to shine a light on some common situations where waiting feels unbearable so we can approach them with a fresh perspective.

Now, let me share a simple reframing technique that has helped me not only endure but grow through some of life's toughest moments: an ugly divorce that led to an embarrassing foreclosure, being laid off from a six-figure job while trying to build my business from scratch, and battling debilitating health issues that tested me physically, emotionally, and spiritually—and yes, some things that only me and God will ever know about. I want to assure you that it's worth the read.

I understand firsthand how waiting patiently can be hard. I thought I was a good person and that I was doing everything—well, most things—right. I was very active in the church and had faith in God. So, why did I have to be punished? Why did I have to watch those around me live a happy life (or so I thought) while I lost everything? I started to question whether the promises He made me would ever come to pass. I was waiting on God to change my situation.

However, as life went on, I began to realize that things weren't as they seemed. This realization marked a major paradigm shift for me. While I was waiting on God, He was waiting on me.

Fast forward to the present, as I am commissioned to write this book, I struggle with completing the task because other things are fighting for my attention. I'm asking God about the next steps He wants me to take in certain areas of my life and the direction for my business. Yet, He has already commissioned me to complete this book by a deadline and to finish one other task. Why does anything else matter at the moment? Clearly, He knows the effect that completing these two tasks will have on the other answers I am seeking. Once again, "While I was waiting on God, He was waiting on me."

We often overlook that while we are waiting, others are waiting on us, too. Our decisions influence not only our own progress but also the progress of those around us. They are waiting for us to share our stories, start that business, or simply say thank you and acknowledge their sacrifices. So, ask yourself: Who is waiting for me to take action?

What people—and God—are truly waiting on is our development and maturation, the very process we often wish to fast-forward or skip entirely. But this journey of growth and self-discovery is essential, not just for our own fulfillment but for the profound impact we're meant to have on the world around us.

With this perspective, let's challenge some common misconceptions about the so-called "waiting game" and uncover the deeper purpose hidden in those moments of anticipation. Together, we'll explore how to approach waiting with intention and transformation, turning it into an opportunity for growth and alignment with our ultimate purpose.

There is a time for everything,

and a season for every activity under the heavens:

a time to be born and a time to die,

a time to plant and a time to uproot,

a time to kill and a time to heal,

a time to tear down and a time to build,

a time to weep and a time to laugh,

a time to mourn and a time to dance,

a time to scatter stones and a time to gather them,

a time to embrace and a time to refrain from embracing,

a time to search and a time to give up,

a time to keep and a time to throw away,

a time to tear and a time to mend,

a time to be silent and a time to speak,

a time to love and a time to hate,

a time for war and a time for peace.

Ecclesiastes 3: 1 – 8 (NIV)

Chapter One

Waiting Is Inevitable

I used to despise waiting. Whether it was for the bus, an important phone call, the results of an interview, or even the inevitable punishment from my mom after she read the teacher's comments about me being too talkative on my report card, waiting felt like a grueling waste of time. The minutes stretched into eternity, and the uncertainty gnawed at me. But over the years, I discovered something that completely changed my perspective and transformed the way I view those seemingly endless moments of anticipation.

Why do we get upset about things we know are inevitable? It's one thing to be caught off guard, but it's another to be fully aware that something is likely to occur. For example, in winter, snow is expected—the kind of snow no one wants to drive in. In spring, flowers bloom, triggering those unbearable allergies that make you want to scratch your eyes out and trade in your nose. Summer brings heat, along with heat rash and sunburn. Fall brings falling leaves, which seem to gather in abundance around our house in the cul-de-sac. This pattern holds true if you live in a place that experiences all four seasons. Even if not, I'm sure you've become accustomed to your home's weather patterns.

Here's one conclusion I've come up with: *we are always fighting for control, whether it is against the things that we know might happen or the things we fear might.* And yet, when we are faced with the inevitable, like the weather, we still find the audacity to complain, as if our frustration could do something about it. It's as though opposing the uncontrollable somehow gives us a false sense of power when, in truth, it only drains us of peace.

Take the above example of the weather. Did you notice that each statement following each season had a negative connotation? Despite the beauty associated with each season, we tend to focus on what we dislike, especially when it's our least favorite season.

Not only do we desire to control things beyond our reach and outcomes, but we also want to control the timing of when we think they should happen. Our inability to control outcomes often leads to anxiety and stress. We get anxious when we don't know how things will turn out, and the more we worry, the more stressed we become.

Understanding the biology behind our stress can shed light on why we react this way. When we experience anxiety, our brain's amygdala (limbic system), which is responsible for processing emotions, kicks into high gear. It sends out an alarm that triggers the "fight or flight" response. Imagine it like a smoke detector going off in your house—sometimes it's a real fire, but sometimes it's just those eggs that you forgot were boiling while you became distracted by five other things. Your brain then floods your body with adrenaline and cortisol, the stress hormones. This was great when we were cave dwellers running from a T-Rex or a saber-toothed tiger, but not so much when we were just waiting for a bus or an important phone call.

As this happens, our heart rate increases, our breathing becomes shallow, and our muscles tense up. These physical changes are your body gearing up to handle a threat. However, when there's no immediate danger, these responses can make you feel jittery and uneasy. This is the essence of anxiety.

Think about it. What percentage of situations is this response actually necessary for? Unless you live in a very dangerous area or work in a very life-threatening environment, probably not many. During my middle school and high school years, I was constantly in this mode. I had acquaintances and friends who were getting brutally injured or even killed. So, you can only imagine what I was going through. I sometimes didn't even want to walk a certain way home or catch certain buses at certain times because of this. That's understandable, but as I am no longer in those types of situations, that response no longer serves me. But I became accustomed to it, and then, unfortunately, those series of events triggered others.

Anxiety then triggers worry. Your mind starts to spin scenarios of what might happen, often focusing on the worst possible outcomes. It's like having a constant "What if?" machine running in your head. This persistent worry keeps your brain and body on high alert, which leads to stress.

Stress is the body's way of responding to any kind of demand or threat. Don't get me wrong—there's good stress and bad stress. I prefer to call them helpful stressors and unhelpful stressors. Helpful stressors, also known as eustress, come into play when you're working toward a goal or striving to meet a meaningful deadline. This type of stress triggers the release of dopamine, the reward hormone, which keeps you motivated, focused, and engaged. You tap into what feels like your optimal performance—a state often referred to as "The Peak."

However, staying in this zone for too long or pushing beyond it comes at a cost. Your body begins releasing higher levels of cortisol, the stress hormone responsible for the "fight-or-flight" response. While short bursts of cortisol can help you deal with immediate challenges, prolonged exposure drains your energy and takes a toll on your body. Think of it like leaving your phone's flashlight on or running 20 apps in the background—it depletes your battery quickly. Over time, this can lead to fatigue, headaches, digestive issues, disrupted sleep, and a weakened immune system. Emotionally, it can manifest as irritability, anxiety, depression, and ultimately burnout.

This cycle of stress and effort can be understood through the FLY Performance Curve (included in the Resources section). Inspired by Yerkes-Dodson's foundational work, this adapted graph illustrates the relationship between stress and performance. It reveals how helpful stress propels you into the Peak Zone, where you are focused and motivated, but also shows the risks of crossing into the Overwhelmed Zone, where fatigue and exhaustion take hold, and eventually, the Burnout Zone, where shutdown and breakdown occur.

Understanding where you fall on the FLY Performance Curve can help you recognize the importance of balance. Learning to manage stress—by embracing rest, patience, and intentional recovery—not only protects your mental health but preserves your overall well-being.

Even the Bible speaks directly to the burden of worry: *"Worry weighs a person down; an encouraging word cheers a person up" (Proverbs 12:25).* This powerful truth reminds us of the heavy toll anxiety takes and the uplifting effect of shifting our mindset. When you learn to accept that some things are beyond your control, you begin to break free from this cycle. Instead of allowing anxiety and stress to dominate, focus on what you can control and release what you cannot. This simple yet profound shift in perspective can be life-changing.

Let me share a story that perfectly illustrates this struggle between impatience and patience.

I love the familiar story of the gentleman who was invited to go to a restaurant by a well-known chef. The gentleman and his wife were seated at a table near the back and were given a menu from which they ordered their food. They became impatient as they watched others, who were seated after them, receive their food before them. After some time had passed, he summoned the waiter over with great irritation, demanding to know why everyone else's food had come out and not theirs. The waiter then explained that because they were special guests of the chef, the chef was personally making something very special for them that wasn't on the menu. Have you ever found yourself growing impatient, only to realize later that the wait was worth it? I know I have!

When I was waiting for a job offer that seemed to take forever, I learned to focus on the skills I could improve in the meantime. That period of waiting turned out to be one of the most productive times of my life.

While wanting to grow closer to God and gain a deeper understanding of His Word, I committed to reading the entire Bible in a year. During this journey, I encountered two Hebrew words for hope—Yakhal (yaw-khal') and Qavah (kaw-vah')—that resonated deeply with me. They weren't just abstract concepts;

they were profound reminders of the waiting process and its purpose. These words became particularly relevant to my journey and the lessons I share in this book. Yakhal invites us to wait expectantly and with quiet confidence, trusting that what we are waiting for will arrive in its due season. It's the kind of hope that allows us to find peace, even in the uncertainty of the moment.

But then there's Qavah, which carries the tension of waiting—like a rope pulled tight, stretched to its limits, yet still holding firm. It reminds us that waiting isn't always easy or comfortable. It can stretch our faith, our patience, and even our understanding of what's possible. Yet, it's in this stretching that we build resilience and strength, preparing ourselves for what's to come.

In the end, *learning to wait patiently is about trust—trusting that the right things will come at the right time and that every waiting period has a purpose.*

There are so many points to pull from the story of the gentlemen at the restaurant. We will talk about this from two perspectives: *the impatient perspective and the patient perspective.*

"Then, turning to his disciples, Jesus said, "That is why I tell you not to worry about everyday life—whether you have enough food to eat or enough clothes to wear. For life is more than food, and your body more than clothing. Look at the ravens. They don't plant or harvest or store food in barns, for God feeds them. And you are far more valuable to him than any birds! Can all your worries add a single moment to your life? And if worry can't accomplish a little thing like that, what's the use of worrying over bigger things? "Look at the lilies and how they grow. They don't work or make their clothing, yet Solomon in all his glory was not dressed as beautifully as they are. And if God cares so wonderfully for flowers that are here today and thrown into the fire tomorrow, he will certainly care for you. Why do you have so little faith? And don't be concerned about what to eat and what to drink. Don't worry about such things. These things dominate the thoughts of unbelievers all over the world, but your Father already knows your needs. Seek the Kingdom of God above all else, and he will give you everything you need."

Luke 12:22-31 (NLT)

Chapter Two

Two Perspectives

"P atience is a virtue" is a common saying that suggests being patient is a commendable trait. So, if patience is virtuous, what does that say about being impatient? Even now, as you read this book, do you want to hurry up and reap the perceived rewards by just skipping to the part that's going to help you work on waiting patiently? Or are you willing to take it all in—pausing, seeing yourself in what's been said, and formulating your own methods of how you can be better? *True rewards come from engaging fully with the process, not just the outcome.*

"Impatience: The Enemy Amidst the Noise"

Reflecting on the gentleman's encounter at the restaurant, many people might default to comments like:

"Well, I would've been mad, too. All the waiter had to do was periodically update them."

"It's the chef's fault. He should've told them he was going to make something special that would take time when he first invited them."

From my hangry folks (those who get angry when they're hungry—like me): "They should've offered some free appetizers or something. Did they bring out the bread?"

From my "spirited" folks: "They should've kept the drinks coming, which would've put them right at ease."

If you said, "Exactly!" to any of these, this book is definitely for you! Here's the challenge with this perspective. Even if one or all of these actions had been taken, would that have guaranteed the gentleman's patience? The answer is "No." And I just heard your rebuttal: "Nothing in life is guaranteed." Thank you so much for proving my point. Since nothing in life is guaranteed, and we can't control the outcome, what is the only thing we can control? *Our responses to situations are within our control.*

When we are anxious about the outcome, we start developing our own expectations, which leads to even more anxiety. This heightened anxiety often stems from our lack of trust in the process. Impatience develops when we feel like our needs or wishes are being ignored, creating a vicious cycle of frustration and stress.

From the impatient perspective, the couple was frustrated because they saw others receiving their meals while they continued to wait. They assumed that something was wrong or unfair. They didn't understand that their wait was for something extraordinary. This impatience could have completely ruined their dining experience had they not been reassured.

How often do we, in our impatience, miss out on the beauty of what's being prepared for us? We focus on what others are getting, feeling overlooked and neglected. This impatience creates unnecessary stress and dissatisfaction.

Patience: Virtue in the Silence

Reflecting on this story, I see parallels in my own life. Waiting is an inevitable part of our journeys, whether we're waiting for a job, a relationship, or a breakthrough. It's natural to want things to happen on our timetable, but life doesn't always work that way. Hardly ever, actually!

For example, when I was waiting on the results of my 15-year-old daughter's breast biopsy. There was a tug-of-war between my faith in God and the harsh reality that cancer had made unwelcome appearances in our family before. To make matters worse, I didn't know much about her father's family history.

I remember when she came to me and said, "Mom, I feel a lump in my breast." Thank God it's not physically possible for our hearts to drop into other places of our bodies because I would've been in serious trouble. I don't know how my heart would've been able to do its job while existing in my stomach.

Trying my best not to show how mortified I really was, I responded calmly, "Really? Can you show me?" Normally quite timid about revealing her body, she pulled her sports bra to the side and guided me right to it. As I touched it and felt the size, what I thought was humanly impossible felt extremely possible. "Does it hurt or feel sensitive?" I asked inquisitively. She responded nonchalantly, "No."

"Well, since today is Saturday, I will call first thing Monday morning to see if we can get it looked at." She responded unbothered, "Okay." As she walked away, I added, "Let me know if it starts to bother you." "Yes, ma'am," she reassured.

Those two days felt like an eternity. But I knew that worrying for an "eternity" wouldn't benefit either of us or anyone who would be in my presence. I took this time to educate myself on what to look for and understand the difference between a benign and a cancerous tumor. I also used this time to lean even more heavily into my conversations with God, meditation, and ensuring I checked up on how my daughter was processing everything.

On Monday morning, at 8:00 am, I was able to get a same-day appointment for my daughter with a physician's assistant, who speculated that it was benign based on the feeling but wanted to confirm with an ultrasound. We managed to get a same-day appointment with the radiologist, and they, too, speculated that it was benign, which was later confirmed with a biopsy that it indeed was benign.

I've found that embracing patience and trusting the process can transform the waiting period into a time of growth and preparation. And if you are anything like me, it will also help strengthen your relationship with God. It's not easy, but shifting our perspective can make all the difference.

As you continue through this book, I encourage you to think about the areas in your life where you're struggling to wait. What can you learn from the waiting process? How can you shift your focus from impatience to patience?

Jim Rohn once said, "You can't change the seasons or the time, but you can change yourself." This wisdom reminds us that while we can't control the timing of life's events, we can choose how we respond to them. *Remember, waiting is inevitable, but how we wait is a choice.* Choose to wait while trusting that what's being prepared for you is worth the wait.

Let's explore this journey together, embracing the waiting periods as opportunities for growth and transformation. At the end of the gentleman's story, some people might default to comments like:

"The gentleman should've asked some questions before getting upset."

"I would've been embarrassed once I found out the chef was doing something special."

"I hope he learned his lesson before flying off the handle next time."

"I wonder what the chef made for them?"

These perspectives and the previous ones highlight a critical contrast. *While impatience breeds frustration, anxiety, and missed opportunities, patience cultivates trust, growth, and a deeper appreciation for life's journey.* You have the power and free will to choose which perspective to adopt; the choice is entirely yours, and it can shape the trajectory of your growth and fulfillment.

As we move forward, we will go deeper into how the stages of the butterfly's life cycle offer profound yet practical insights into navigating the seasons of life with intention and purpose. This approach has transformed my understanding of growth, and I believe it can do the same for you. Let's take flight into this journey together, embracing every moment as an opportunity to thrive.

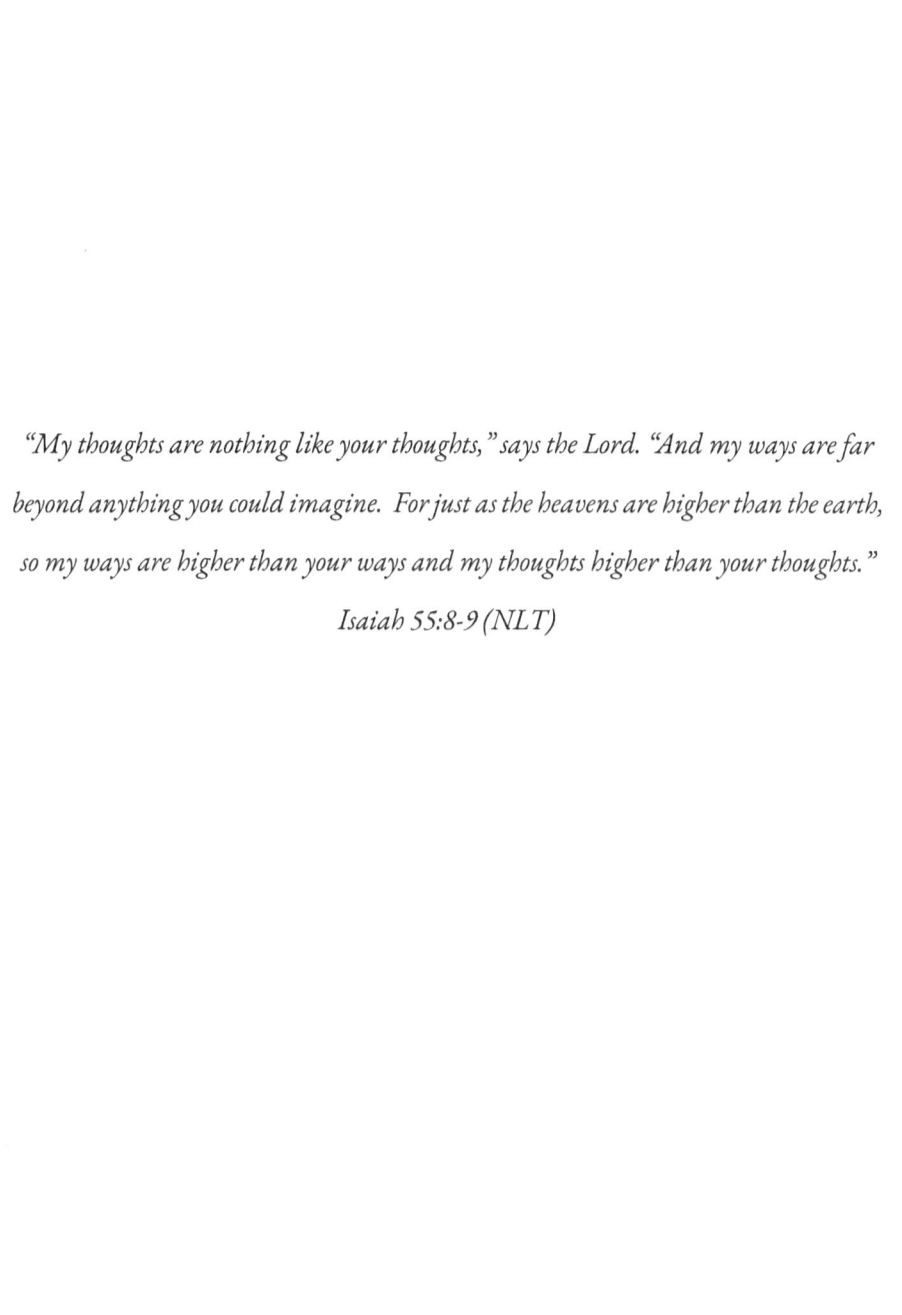

"My thoughts are nothing like your thoughts," says the Lord. "And my ways are far beyond anything you could imagine. For just as the heavens are higher than the earth, so my ways are higher than your ways and my thoughts higher than your thoughts."

Isaiah 55:8-9 (NLT)

Chapter Three

Butterfly Obsession

There has always been something alluring about butterflies to me. Not just the beauty, but I've felt a deep connection to them, even during the caterpillar stage. I'm so captivated by them that I've often yearned to be cocooned with them, enveloped in their transformative embrace. So, choosing to have them tattooed on different places on my body only makes sense, right?

I can remember when my older sisters, Leshia and Danna, came home with their first tattoos. Leshia was seven years older than me; she got her name in this beautiful cursive writing. Danna, five years older than me, had gotten her daughter's name, Nicosia, in a beautiful, enchanting font as well. I remember how their newly stained body parts were a proclamation of their adulthood. At least, that's what I thought. It was funny watching their covert attempts to avoid the backlash they would more than likely receive from our very religious mother. It was our sisters' secret.

Ever since then, I just knew that my first tattoo would be a majestically shaped and multi-colored butterfly. So, five years later, when I turned 18 and 1 day old, was the age requirement for this popular hole-in-the-wall establishment, my sisters took me to Tattoo Charlie's, in Downtown Baltimore. I remember barely sleeping the night before. The thought of a steel needle piercing through the top 5 layers of my skin from 50 to 3,000 cycles per minute wasn't what was causing me to toss and turn in my sleep. But it was the butterflies in my stomach thinking about how "officially FLY" I was going to be. I didn't care about the pain they described; I was excited to join the "Sisters' Secret Tatted Club." Of course, by this time, my sisters had several. Our brother, Josef, was ineligible to join the club, not just because he was a boy but because he was only eight at the time.

As I sat in the small, dimly lit waiting room, flipping through the many pages of butterflies, I could hear the buzzing song of the artists stroking their canvases. As I gazed at hundreds of options, different shapes and sizes, simplistic to complex, grayscale to "I didn't know there were so many colors," I was waiting for one to really speak to me. I turned the page, and without it saying anything at all, it spoke to me in ways that I couldn't imagine. I had finally found it – the perfect, majestically shaped, and multi-colored butterfly tattoo.

The vibrant hues made it come to life right there on the page. The left underwing was exposed and arched as if it was stretching, waking up from a peaceful night's rest, revealing the fragile yet resilient crescent moon-shaped body nestled within. Staged midflight, a quarter of the right wing accompanied the left as if to attest freedom and movement but frozen in time.

Between these majestic wings, a V-shaped opening invites exploration, a glimpse into a world of possibilities. Here, I envisioned a gold crown hovering gracefully over the antennae like a celestial halo. The antennae, extended upward, then outward, curled forward, ever alert, as if it wanted to remain on the correct frequency and be attuned to the whispers of the universe.

And yet, it was the wings that unlocked the keys to my heart. From the core, pointing outward toward the edges, delicate sunflower-shaped petals adorn the wings. Their hues reminiscent of sun-kissed meadows and azure skies. Reds, yellows, and blues intertwined together like an intimate, extravagant, choreographed dance. Each shade bleeding into the next like a watercolor masterpiece unfolding, like a spilled cup of water seeping into the thirsty earth, saturating every pore with vibrant life and color. Along the edges was brushed with prominent punches of royal purple.

This tattoo was going to be more than just mere ink on my skin; it was destined to be a manifestation of intention and vulnerability, a declaration of purpose intertwined with openness to the unknown. It would be a reminder that beauty lies not only in perfection but also in the journey of becoming. It was settled! So, I thought.

The tattoo artist called me back to the chair and asked, "So, what letters did you pick?" Confused by his line of questioning, "I'm sorry, letters?" "Yes," he said. "Your sisters said it's only right that your first tattoo be a name because that was theirs, and plus, they are paying for it." How could I argue the case that was presented before me? Needless to say, my first tattoo was my nickname on my left arm in Gothic Old English-style font. I was a bit disappointed that I couldn't take my winged soulmate home with me.

However, I made sure to return to Mr. Bear—yes, that was his name—just one day later, determined to claim my winged soulmate. At 18 years and 2 days old,

I paid the ransom for my majestically shaped and multi-colored butterfly tattoo. Oracle, as I later named her, found her new home on my back left shoulder blade. Though her vibrant hues looked more alive on paper, my melanin made a valiant effort to catch up with her breathtaking presence. Each deliberate stroke of Mr. Bear's needle seemed like a small attempt to teleport her from the white pages of the butterfly book to her rightful place.

Though his intentions were pure, her new sanctuary didn't do her justice, as my skin couldn't quite replicate her vibrant colors. But it didn't matter, because now, we were one, even though she wasn't my first.

Now, fast forward twenty-two years later, on my fortieth birthday, my obsession with butterflies was revealed, and it was so comforting yet invigorating. It all made so much sense! On the surface, it's easy to say it's transformation and the metamorphosis, but it's so much deeper than that.

Embracing this life-changing lesson has helped me personally manage and oftentimes avoid what would be considered stressful or anxiety-filled situations.

If you had tools that could help you in those two common areas alone, how much of a difference would that make in your life?

Well, I want to share with you the revelation that I received and how I've used this concept, theory, and enlightenment in my coaching business to change the lives of hundreds, if not thousands (thanks to the internet) at this point.

As we move through the stages of the butterfly's life cycle in this book, I will share more about how the challenges I've faced led to deeper struggles and, ultimately, profound growth. Each stage has taught me invaluable lessons.

While each stage of the butterfly's life cycle reflects a specific phase of transformation, the stories I'll share don't always unfold chronologically. Instead, they explore how the themes of each stage—vulnerability, growth, transformation, and purpose—have shown up in different areas of my life at different times. My hope is that this approach helps you see the interconnectedness of your own journey.

The Butterfly Life Cycle:
The Stages of Waiting

Chapter Four

The Egg Stage

"Before I formed you in the womb I knew you, before you were born, I set you apart; I appointed you as a prophet to the nations."

Jeremiah 1:5 (NIV)

Why Isn't It Happening Yet?

Impatient Perspective

Characteristics: *beginning, fragile, vulnerable, small, insignificant, unnoticeable, unsure, undeveloped, and exposed.*

W hen I asked people to describe what they felt the egg stage of the butterfly life cycle represented, their responses often shared a common thread. *"The egg stage seems like a beginning where everything is so small and undeveloped,"* one person remarked, their lips curling into a faint smile that didn't quite reach their eyes—a mix of nostalgia and acceptance. "It represents being exposed and vulnerable, with no means of defense," they added, eyebrows lifting as if the thought alone made them feel defenseless.

Another person furrowed their brows, eyes darting to the side as if trying to grasp the abstractness of their own words. "It feels like the start of a long, slow process, and there's no guarantee of success," they said, their voice blending hope and doubt. Someone else let out a small sigh, their gaze dropping momentarily, before stating,

"The egg stage seems so small and insignificant, almost invisible in the grand scheme of things." It was as if they, too, felt the sting of being unseen.

Then there was the person who spoke as if reciting a line from a script they didn't believe in: "The egg stage symbolizes undeveloped potential—just waiting there, no action." Their tone was flat, yet their furrowed brow betrayed the weight of their own experience with "waiting." Each description painted a vivid picture of fragility, hesitation, and uncertainty as if the egg stage were a holding pattern for dreams yet to be realized.

What surprised me most wasn't just the words they used but how easily the conversation spilled over into personal revelations. Some began recounting moments where they felt caught in their own egg stage—anxious, unsure, and stuck. Others opened a floodgate of memories, describing past experiences with such clarity that I could almost see their stories unfolding. It was as if the very act of naming this stage pulled back a curtain, revealing unspoken fears and hidden vulnerabilities.

What struck me was how rarely anyone spoke of the egg stage in a positive light. I could count on one hand the number of people who saw it as anything other than fragile or insignificant. Yet, as someone who has learned to view this stage through a different lens, I couldn't help but wonder: Were these rare optimists onto something? Were they privy to a truth that the rest of us often overlook?

After all, who wants to be described as fragile in a world that celebrates strength and resilience? Who willingly admits to being undeveloped when progress and accomplishment are the gold standards of success? And let's be honest—how many of us truly embrace beginnings when they so often highlight how far we still have to go?

Yet, perhaps those who view the egg stage positively have uncovered a hidden gem. They recognize the quiet strength nestled within fragility, the limitless potential in what is yet to develop, and the immense value of starting anew. They see beauty not in the final product but in the process of becoming.

I can't say I've always belonged to this enlightened group. Beginnings used to feel daunting to me—frustrating, even. But reflecting on these perceptions of the egg stage led me to think about the early stages of relationships, starting a business, and navigating health challenges. In those moments, the sense of vulnerability felt all too familiar. Yet, what I couldn't see then was that those fragile beginnings were brimming with possibility, waiting to unfold in ways I couldn't yet imagine.

The Seed of Us

Relationship

From what I can recall, growing up, I've never had good examples of healthy, long-lasting relationships. My mom and dad were both married to other individuals when I was conceived, leaving my first line of defense nonexistent. I never met my maternal grandparents, and although my paternal grandparents were married for almost 60 years until death parted them, I didn't have the pleasure of meeting them until I was 20. Even then, the distance was an issue; they lived three states away, an eight-hour drive—so I wasn't around them often enough to use them as examples. Yes, there's a lot to unpack there --but those stories deserve their own books, maybe even a trilogy.

Without "good examples," I decided, in all of my wisdom (yes, the little I had), to do some "reverse engineering." I thought I could use the flawed examples I had, figure out what they did wrong, and do the complete opposite! Clearly, my reverse engineering skills weren't skilled enough. As I navigated my twenties and early thirties, I realized that relationships were far more complex than my poor, inexperienced mind could comprehend. Picking apart peoples' relationships and trying to apply those lessons to my life wasn't the answer either!

At the age of 34, I had been officially experiencing life after death—I mean divorce—for two years. I was also jetlag-free for five months off the ride of a 16-month serious relationship that was going nowhere fast. Despite these setbacks, each failed relationship built my resilience. As I navigated these potential "I can do bad by myself" experiences, I actually found myself in a sweet spot in life. I was embracing being FLY (First Loving Yourself), confident, and achieving my goals left and right. Most importantly, I was content with being by myself.

I knew I still desired to be a wife, but not at the expense of settling. I wanted my daughters to see nothing but the best example of a healthy partnership, and most importantly, I didn't want to lose myself...AGAIN. Honestly, I was in no rush! Knowing this, I formed a hard shell and had my guard up—WAAAYYY UP!

And then came this guy, not just any guy, but this man—no, this "alien" whose mental, physical, spiritual, emotional, and financial intelligence abruptly challenged my self-proclaimed contentment. Not in a cocky way, very subtly—and now that I understand his behind-the-scenes actions, quite unintentionally. His character, charisma, confidence, and consistency slowly chipped away at that protective shell, creating cracks until I was exposed. "Wait, is this the right move?"

I could still hear the hateful words from *The Marriage of Christmas Past*: "No man is ever going to want a woman with three kids!" After all this time, who would've thought those words would rear their ugly head to haunt me? Especially at such a vulnerable time. I mean, this was the beginning of something that seemed so pure and divine. Though reeking of stale bad breath, were those harsh words there to sober me up? "I don't want to introduce my daughters to another relationship that isn't going to last." While it also felt so right, I also felt...unsure.

I became accepting of the possibilities when I acknowledged the fact that *there must always be a beginning before you get to an ending.* There was so much comfort and a sense of peace within that realization when I chose to—JUST BE PRESENT.

Being present allowed me to see things for what they were and turn a blind eye to what they could be. Every time I experienced a wave of would-be doubt or anxiety, it was because I was looking too much into the future. I wasn't sure what the future held, but I did know that I loved the way he held me. I didn't know whether or not he would do something tomorrow that would make me cry. But on that present day, I appreciated that he knew the right things to say and do to make me smile.

He made me feel safe, like a priceless jewel, guarded by a fortress of unwavering devotion, all while diligently navigating through the aftermath of his own divorce disaster. His unwavering support and gentle strength provided a sanctuary amidst the chaos, allowing me to trust and heal in ways I never thought possible.

Over the past 10 years, we often reflect on how pivotal the beginning moments were with us merging and thriving happily together. He says, "When I felt like I was drowning, God threw me a life-saver—and it was you. You were patient and understanding because just a few short years prior, you had been through it, too." I shared with him that though I might have been his life-saver, I yearned to be caught and held onto, like someone's life depended on it. Not in an exhaustive codependent way but in an appreciative, admirable, and affirmative-type way. In the beginning, we both understood that the positions we were in were delicate but promising because we were deliberate about budding together.

As I reflect on those delicate yet promising beginnings in my relationship, I can't help but think about how the early stages of anything—be it love, career, or even self-discovery—require the same patience and trust in the process. Just as I had to embrace the uncertainties and joys of my budding relationship, I found myself navigating a similar path when it came to shaping my professional identity.

For me, the journey of entrepreneurship didn't begin with a grand vision or a polished business plan. In fact, it started much earlier, long before I even knew what entrepreneurship was—back in a time when dreams were innocent and unshaped and possibilities felt endless. It was during these formative years that the seeds of who I would become were planted, even if I didn't yet recognize their potential.

Endless Possibilities

Entrepreneurship

When I was about five years old, I remember being asked the world's most common question by adults: "What do you want to be when you grow up?" My answers varied at different stages of my life. At five, I wanted to be a model. I took so much pride in my appearance and often got in trouble for changing my clothes every time they got a bit dirty. Living in South Carolina, where everything around me was dirt and grass, made this a serious issue. I loved being outdoors and playing, so you can imagine my mother's frustration.

As I grew older, my ambitions shifted with my experiences. At one point, I wanted to be a singer. When I was six, now attending an elementary school in Florida, I dressed up as Lena Horne and lip-synced to "The Wiz – Believe In Yourself" during a Black History Month program. I remember seeing that photo tucked away in a large photo album that my mom stocked with my life's photos. It was so surreal. I had on this pink satin church dress, and my long, black, thick hair was straightening-comb-Blue Magic-pressed.

By the time I reached twelve, another talent emerged that would carry me through my teenage years. I "fell into" doing hair. When we moved to Baltimore, Maryland, it was a skill I had to learn because I wanted to look cute, and my aunt, who was going to cosmetology school and living with us at the time, seemed to have enough time to do everyone else's hair but mine. Plus, my mom, being a single mother with three children in a new state, had more important things to do with her money. With my teenage, immature, selfish way of thinking, I wasn't initially in agreement with that logic. However, I realized that my energy would be best used focusing on the things I could control. So, I learned how to do my own hair, then others started taking notice. This newfound skill quickly turned into a profitable venture.

In high school, I would set up my salon in the bathrooms, before and after school, between classes, and even during lunch. Reflecting on it and saying it out loud now sounds pretty gross, but we did what we had to do. The most requested hairstyle was finger waves, and I could do them on just about anyone's hair type in about five minutes. I charged $15 per person, and if you wanted a French roll or a pre-rodded ponytail, it was $20. Girls would be walking around with the thick, brown Ampro Pro Styl gel all down the sides of their faces, where I extended the exaggerated 'S' wave.

Reflecting on this entrepreneurial spirit, I realize how much it shaped my understanding of work and creativity. The way that I could wield two metal-tailed rat tail combs was magical. Normally, most would come back the next day, ensuring the style was dry, to get the finger waves lifted. I made pretty good money, too! I had walking-talking mannequins, and the exaggerated 'S' was my calling card. But

I never considered it as entrepreneurship. Actually, I didn't even know what that was. This phase was a whirlwind of creativity and hustle. Each hairstyle I perfected was a small victory, a testament to my resourcefulness and promising talent.

My ignorance of entrepreneurship stemmed from the limited career advice I received. "Graduate from high school, go to college, get a good ole post office or government job, and then retire," were the marching orders I was given by the older generation. My mom, though having many phenomenal talents like sewing and cooking, has always worked for someone else. So did the other few adults I was consistently exposed to. Despite these limited career views, high school offered me a glimpse of a different future.

In high school, I saw small glimpses of having a career in performing arts as I studied music, acting, and dancing. I was in the gospel choir, concert choir, and jazz ensemble, and I participated in fashion shows, plays, and liturgical dance. I was also in the marching band and participated in and ran the performing arts department for a while at my church.

But then came the daunting task of deciding my future. It was time to start applying for college.

"What is your major?," the counselor asked.

"My major?"

The only time I met with the counselor was when I got put out of class for debating—they called it arguing—with the teachers, missing one too many days of school, fighting a few times, and when there were rumors of me being involved with an older man—seven years older to be exact. Nothing happened, as he wasn't affiliated with the school system at all. Yet, another series of books for another day. I was not prepared to choose what I would be doing for the rest of my life. Whose idea was that? The pressure to decide my future at such a young age felt overwhelming and unfair.

As she handed me a plastic bag, she instructed me to put a bunch of colorful pamphlets for potential schools in it. It felt like she was getting rid of yesterday's newspapers off of a stand. Then, I found myself making room for the 75-page packet, photocopied front-and-back, with small-smeared font from being copied way too many times, which contained a list of possible majors.

As if I didn't feel undeveloped and unsure enough, I was given an unforgivable deadline to make this life-changing decision in just a couple of weeks. "Are you kidding me?" How was I expected to do this? I was still discovering who I was, let alone what career path I wanted to follow.

Though my sisters had their degrees, neither of them seemed to be elated by their career choices. My mom hadn't gotten her first of two degrees until years later. Should I follow this charted path of going to college, or should I explore this unspoken, uncharted course of doing something I was good at, making my own schedule, in demand, and earning good money fairly quickly?

I may not have a choice. Though I'd had my fair share of mishaps in high school, I was an okay student. Not because I wasn't smart but because I really didn't apply myself. At that time, there were other things that were more important. What's more important than getting good grades in school? The first priority was making sure you weren't getting bullied, banked (severely beaten), stabbed, or shot just because of where you lived or who you hung around.

Things like making sure you were in at least one "in" crowd to minimize the probability of your first priority happening were crucial. So, this uncharted course might be my only option.

And then, unexpectedly, I received a letter...

"Congratulations, you've been accepted into The College of Notre Dame of Maryland for the upcoming Fall/Spring 98/99 Semester. We are delighted to welcome you to our Computer Science Program."

As I read that acceptance letter, I couldn't help but feel a spark of possibility—a glimmer of hope that perhaps this uncharted course might lead somewhere meaningful. Yet, even as I stood at the brink of a new chapter in my life, there was a deeper, more personal journey unfolding within me. It was one I couldn't ignore, even as I tried to focus on academics and career paths.

Beneath the surface of these decisions about my future, I was beginning to confront a challenge I didn't fully understand at the time: my health. Like many young women, I had grown up seeing certain struggles normalized, but as my body started to send louder signals, I realized that something wasn't quite right. The same uncertainty that marked my academic and career journey was mirrored in my physical well-being.

Unseen Beginnings

Health

I was raised with a strong emphasis on ensuring my soul was right with God. We went to church almost every day of the week—or at least it felt like it. Whether it was for an actual service like Bible study, Sunday morning worship, or communion, or for preparing for a service through meetings for the many ministries my mom, sisters, brother, and I were involved in, choir rehearsals, cleaning the building, or cooking the food to be served after an all-day service, church was a constant in our lives. This is why I adopted the belief that our soul and relationship with God were paramount in living this ***human experience*** called life. The irony, right?

Some believe our spirits exist beyond physical birth and death, while others think that after death, we don't exist again until Christ raises us. I don't wish to debate any of these beliefs. This is admittedly a rhetorical question, but if our souls are our primary focus, why do we inhabit these 'meatsuits'? There must be a reason we have both, right? To stay on point, let's direct our energy into acknowledging that since we were given physical bodies—these meatsuits—it's important for us to take great care of them, too.

This realization came to me later in life, but it profoundly changed how I view my body. I learned that neglecting it wasn't an option if I wanted to live a fulfilling life. What role does your physical health play in your life? Have you ever really considered the impact of ignoring the signals of misalignment that it emits, thus causing you to neglect your 'meatsuit'?

I wasn't what would be considered a sickly child. I was quite healthy, never breaking a bone or needing surgery. I don't even recall missing many days of school due to common colds or stomach viruses. However, I do recall the relentless urge to put on sandpaper gloves and furiously scratch my skin raw during my bout with chickenpox. Outside of that, I had a fairly clean bill of health—until I started my menstrual cycle.

When I first got my period, I was 13 years old. Most of my friends had theirs at least a year or two before me. I can recall having the symptoms of cramping, nausea, and fatigue way before the first sign of blood. I thought something was wrong with me. "Why was it taking so long?" I would ask. My mother used to warn me, "When it comes, you will want it to leave." I was so annoyed by how she and the other adults would talk in riddles like we needed a secret decoder wheel to decipher them.

Having your cycle was a big deal for us as young girls. We were told that this was THE indicator of becoming a woman. Why wouldn't we want it to hurry up and grace us with the badge of honor? Do you know what it would mean? It would mean that we are very close to being able to do womanly things like staying up late, wearing makeup and high heels, driving, and not having to worry about going to school, or being bossed around. Little did we know that being a woman entailed more than this, and some of these things would actually remain the same or become even more intense.

After several false alarms and possible spotting sightings, the day came when I got my period. I honestly don't remember the exact day because all the cycles that followed made me wish I had never invited it to come. My menstrual cycle wasn't just a typical milestone; it marked the beginning of a challenging health journey.

When my menstrual cycle began, it was the first hint of the health struggles to come. I started experiencing severe fatigue and heavy bleeding. At first, I didn't think much of it, assuming it was just part of the process of becoming a woman. But as the symptoms worsened, it became clear that something more serious was happening.

This phase would lead to a series of health issues that prompted multiple procedures and surgeries, as well as impact my ability to fulfill a life-long desire of mine. Each of these challenges required me to learn patience and to just trust the process.

Have you ever faced a health challenge that taught you patience? How did it change your perspective on your physical well-being? These early experiences with my health taught me a profound lesson about beginnings: they are often delicate, uncertain, and filled with unseen potential. What initially felt like a challenge beyond my understanding was, in hindsight, a pivotal stage of growth—a compact promise waiting to unfold.

Where Beauty Begins

Patient Perspective

J ust as my relationship, entrepreneurship, and health journeys began with unexpected challenges, we find parallels in nature that teach us about patience and potential. Let's explore the egg stage from a ***patient perspective, which characteristics are: potential, delicate, promising, compact, pivotal, unseen potential, anticipatory, and budding.***

Here's what you need to know about the egg stage. Did you know that female butterflies lay their eggs in places (crevices, underside and top of leaves, and bark) to camouflage and protect them from the weather and predators? Did you also know that they lay them on leaves and stems so that when they hatch, the larvae can immediately begin to feed? Isn't that reassuring? So much forethought goes into when, where, and what the beginning will look like. However, from our vantage point, we often can't see that—at least initially. "Why is that?" ***Often, we are so consumed with our current condition that we ignore our position.***

See, our creator strategically places us where we can immediately benefit from the things, people, and places on our new journey. He already understands what obstacles we will face and has ensured that we will have all that we need to advance to the next stage. Stop waiting on God to rush the egg stage and start seeking the provisions He has made for you to not just survive but thrive. He knew you needed a fresh start with a new identity because the old one wasn't serving you.

The egg holds within it the quiet promise of transformation, embodying the essence of potential, resilience, and the beauty that can emerge from even the seemingly delicate and uncertain beginnings. In my relationship with Rob, this potential was fragile yet undeniable. After a history of failed relationships and a marriage that made me question what love truly meant, stepping into something new with him felt both scary and hopeful. We both knew our positions were delicate, but we were deliberate about nurturing what was budding between us. It's a stage of hidden strength, awaiting the right conditions to unveil its remarkable journey toward becoming a magnificent butterfly.

The egg stage is not just about the beginning; it's about potential—hidden and waiting to be realized. It's a call to hope for what's not yet visible. *"If we already have something, we don't need to hope for it. But if we look forward to something we don't yet have, we must wait patiently and confidently"(Romans 8:24-25 NLT).* Your beginning is filled with promise, even if you can't see it yet. It's about recognizing that every start, no matter how small or seemingly insignificant, holds the blueprint for greatness.

Entrepreneurship carried the same mix of uncertainty and promise. I had no idea what it meant to be an entrepreneur—I didn't even know the word growing up. What I did have was a collection of talents and an unexpected acceptance letter to The College of Notre Dame of Maryland. Surviving high school in my neighborhood often took priority over academics, but that letter became a seed, representing potential I hadn't yet recognized. It set me on a path toward purpose and entrepreneurship, even if I couldn't see it at the time.

When it came to my health, the egg stage revealed things I'd been blind to for years. Raised in a home where spiritual well-being took precedence, ignoring my body felt almost normal. I saw my first period as a symbol of womanhood, not knowing how much it would later disrupt my life. Health challenges, surgeries, and unfulfilled desires forced me to cultivate patience and trust, a process I couldn't control. Those early struggles held a hidden strength that shaped me in ways I didn't fully understand until later.

Before you can become anything, you must first...be. See what I did there? (wink) This underscores the importance of presence and self-awareness as the foundation of growth. Before we take on roles, pursue goals, or embody qualities we aspire to, there's power in simply *being*—grounded, fully ourselves, and connected to our values. In that stillness, we find clarity about who we are, which then informs who we *become*. This aligns well with the idea that transformation begins with self-acceptance and awareness. It's almost like ***"being" is the soil from which everything else grows.***

All Things Have a Beginning

Transformation Truths

The egg stage reminds us that every journey begins somewhere—fragile, unformed, and full of potential. Are you ready to uncover the truths about embracing the beauty and promise of a beginning?

Anticipatory and Budding Potential: During the egg stage, we are in a state of anticipation. We might not see immediate results, but within this tiny form lies the foundation for future growth. Think about times in your life when you started something new—a job, a relationship, a personal project. The beginnings were delicate and filled with promise. It's important to nurture these starts with care and patience.

Camouflage and Protection: Just as butterfly eggs are hidden in safe places, our initial stages are often protected in ways we might not realize. Whether it's the support of loved ones, the guidance of mentors, or the unseen workings of Angels, or the beautifully orchestrating Hands of God, there are protective measures in place to help us grow. Recognize and appreciate these safeguards in your life.

Immediate Nourishment: When butterfly larvae hatch, they are immediately able to feed. Similarly, when we embark on a new journey, we are often provided with the initial resources we need to thrive. It might be the skills we've developed, the networks we've built, or the inner resilience we've cultivated. Trust that you have what you need to begin.

Patience in Potential: The egg stage teaches us the value of patience. Just as the egg must incubate and develop before it can hatch, we, too, must allow time for our potential to unfold. This patience is not passive but active—engaging in self-care, continuous learning, and maintaining a hopeful outlook.

Reflection and Anticipation: Reflect on your own life and identify your egg stages. Ask yourself: What new beginnings am I currently nurturing? How can I protect and nourish them? What provisions have been made for me? What's currently in my environment that's paramount to my survival and growth? What is the egg stage revealing to me? About me?

Affirmation: "I will embrace the anticipation of what's to come, knowing that each stage is a crucial part of my journey."

A Butterfly's Transformation

"My life was a whirlwind. I had many goals and several unfinished projects. Life Coach Von guided me through my whirlwind and provided me with tools that helped me organize my life.

One of the most memorable lessons focused on patience and trusting the process. My impatience and not trusting the process were fueling my whirlwind and negatively affecting my confidence. Now, I break my goals down into tiers with realistic time frames of completion. With my mindset shift and practical application, I've been able to accomplish so much! This allowed me to understand the importance of allowing the goal to form. She showed me that having faith, even when my path is rocky, and believing in myself can help me reach my goal."

~ Charlisa King

Metamorphosis Moment

*The **egg stage** whispers of infinite potential wrapped in the quiet of beginnings. It reminds us that within the smallest seeds of faith lie the foundations of greatness, waiting patiently to be nurtured into existence.*

~ Life Coach Von

Chapter Five

Stage 2: The Caterpillar Stage

Now faith is the substance of things hoped for, the evidence of things not seen.

Hebrews 11:1 (KJV)

This Feels Pointless

Impatient Perspective

Characteristics: ugly, slow, creepy, outcasted, disgusting, pointless, and underdeveloped.

When I asked people to describe their feelings about the larva, commonly known as the caterpillar stage of the butterfly life cycle, their responses often revealed a deep sense of confusion, discomfort, and even disgust.

"Oh, that's the formal name? Larva? Well, the larva stage seems like the ugly phase where everything is so slow and creepy," one person said, reflecting discomfort and repulsion. "It represents being an outcast, something that doesn't belong," they ad ded.

Another person's eyes showed unease and impatience. "It feels like a pointless phase, with no real purpose but to creep people out!" Someone else shook their head in disapproval, expressing a sense of being stuck and unimportant. "To me, that stage seems so disgusting and just in the way. I don't look forward to seeing them in the spring when their long, lanky bodies squirm across the sidewalks. I would purposely step on one if the yucky squishing sound and the gook under my shoe wouldn't bother me."

Unlike the egg stage, no one immediately connected with the caterpillar stage until I asked, "Does this stage resonate with you in any way?" Most paused and looked up and over to the left as if they were reaching for a box of cereal on the top back shelf. Some of them even nodded slowly, accompanied by a thoughtful, drawn-out "Hmmmm?"

Encouraging them to share more openly, I asked, "What are you thinking about?" The common response was that they couldn't seem to get past the caterpillar's unattractive appearance to draw any meaningful connection to their lives. Extracting these thoughts felt like pulling teeth, as no one had anything positive to say about the caterpillar or this stage.

Except for one person who briefly stated, "I guess it has to get ugly before it gets pretty." I took that as a sign he understood this stage was necessary before reaching the adult butterfly stage, even though he didn't know the intricate inner workings.

I couldn't relate to them on this one regarding its ugliness. I've always found caterpillars to be uniquely fascinating. However, I could relate to their initial disconnect, as my appreciation for the caterpillar stage took time to develop. This revelation came once I reflected on the awkward and uncomfortable stages of my own journeys.

Who wants to be described as, or even admit that they are, ugly when it appears the world takes delight in beauty and attractiveness? Who wants to be involved in anything that's slow, as it suggests a lack of efficiency and progress? Who appreciates crawling, as it points to a lack of grace and speed?

Of all the stages, the appreciation for the caterpillar phase is often the most overlooked and undervalued. Caterpillars, with their "weird" appearance and slow movements, lack the immediate allure of butterflies.

Just look at how people described it. To make matters worse, the caterpillar stage is frequently compared unfavorably to the butterfly stage. One person even mentioned that they would step on a caterpillar but sob at the thoughts of an injured butterfly. Yet, what if I told you that what the caterpillar does (or doesn't do) at this stage is essential to the development of the later stages of metamorphosis? The caterpillar, despite its unassuming appearance, is crucial.

In my own life, I've experienced these caterpillar stages. During the early stages of relationships, there's often a period of adjustment where everything feels awkward and uncertain. It's easy to see this phase as unimportant or even uncomfortable, but it's crucial for developing a deep, meaningful connection.

Shedding and Growing Together

Relationship

W hen I first met my husband, his situation wasn't what I, or probably what anyone, would consider ideal. I remember the first time we met—it's actually quite hard to forget, as we now celebrate it every year and have dubbed it our "meetaversary" due to how pivotal it was in the progression of our relationship.

I had been single for six months and was living my best life. I was thriving in my singleness! I wasn't rediscovering or trying to find myself; I was defining the new me, taking ownership of how I wanted to show up in life—not by the standards of the church, my family or friends, my job, or society, but by who I felt God made me to be at that point in time. This time, I didn't fall prey to the common thoughts and behaviors that often accompany being alone.

In the past, I've personally experienced and heard others say things like, "I have to get back to being me," or "I need to find myself," after leaving long-term or serious relationships. We are so used to being with or catering to someone besides ourselves, giving us the false pretenses of being whole or complete, that we lose touch with our individual identities. ***We need to stop looking outside ourselves to fill a void that's within ourselves.***

The trouble with the thought of "I need to find myself" is that we are often looking for someone who no longer exists, causing us to feel stuck and identity-less for extended periods. Instead, if we embrace the idea that everything we experience in life shapes us into a new being—whether we want it to or not—our bounce back will be much quicker, and redefining ourselves will be much easier. This leads to a higher rate of self-acceptance. It's our choice whether we allow these experiences to make us better or worse.

Consider the process of baking a cake. My mom used to make cakes from scratch all the time, and my all-time favorite was red velvet cake. Besides the rich, royal red color, the smell and taste are unforgettable. The moistness of the cake was unparalleled, each bite melting in my mouth like butter. The whipped cream cheese icing was a decadent complement; its tanginess perfectly balanced the sweetness. She would artfully place pecan halves on top, followed by sprinkles of chopped pecans, and dusted with pulverized pecan bits. The texture was a symphony of creaminess and crunch, making each slice a multi-sensory delight.

Every time she made one, I'd be right there, cleaning the bowls and mixers—not by washing them, but by licking them clean, of course, and then with soap and water. I was disappointed when she purchased the really good spatulas that barely left anything behind.

What made me love this cake so much was the way she made it. I studied the ingredients, so when it was time to make it, I knew what she needed. If, for any reason, we didn't have any unsweetened cocoa powder, the chocolatey flavor that is found in a red velvet cake would be absent, turning it into a pink velvet cake with more of a yellow cake flavor. Adding more salt, sugar, buttermilk, or baking soda than the recipe calls for can completely change the taste, texture, or experience. This same concept applies to our lives.

One newly added or subtracted experience makes us a completely different person. And no, you can't just extract what's been added. Once it's baked, it's even more difficult to make adjustments unless you break it down or start from scratch. So, when I say I was thriving, I was walking boldly in the "new me." I had made up in my mind what was acceptable, the boundaries that needed to be set, and the consequences that would be applied if any of those things weren't adhered to. So, you can only imagine what my husband was walking into at that time.

I was so absorbed in my own little world that I didn't even know he was remotely interested in me. We met at a mutual friend's dual celebration, The Brashers, who are now more like family than friends. April was launching her fitness brand, which is how I even became a part of this crowd, and her husband, Khary, was celebrating his birthday, who invited me to the event. I wasn't alone, as I had received approval to bring a couple of friends with me, Kenisha and Niya.

Niya's favorite drink was gin and tonic, and it was my turn to grab a round of drinks, as she normally likes to beat everyone to the punch and make sure glasses never run dry. While standing at the bar, waiting for the bartender to return, a cool, confident, yet inviting voice says, "I like your haircut" while approaching. I believe it was strategic as it was his way of announcing himself without startling me, as my back was turned to the crowd. Glancing over my shoulder, smiling with genuine appreciation, I said, "Thanks!" Getting compliments on my haircut was a very common thing for me.

During that time, very few—I mean very few—women were rockin' mohawks. Even if they were, they weren't doing it like me. Mine was usually bright blonde, short, curly, and faded to perfection like your favorite old-school acid wash jeans, beautifully blended into shaved sides. Not to mention, my dark brown skin complexion and gray eyes made a bold statement of confidence and uniqueness—the contrast was striking. This time, my bright blonde curly mohawk, standing about four inches off my head, was Hot Tamales red.

So, receiving a compliment about my Baltimore barber's work didn't signal, "I'm tryna get to know you." After a very short and polite conversation and finally receiving the drink from the bartender, he wrapped up the conversation with, "The drink is on me, and save me a dance." Again, appreciative but clueless that there was the slightest interest, I said, "Thanks and ok." I returned to my friends after about a 10-minute bar run, handing Niya her drink, "This cute guy bought me—well, you—a drink." Kenisha gave me the eye, "What guy?" As I scanned the room, I couldn't seem to find him to point him out. "Let me find out you have an admirer already," Niya said. "Hmmmhm," Kenisha voted. "Nahhh, it wasn't like that," I excl aimed.

As the night progressed, he happened to find me and my friends and introduced himself. I was sure to whisper with my eyes to my friends, "This is the guy." As the space was intimate and the music wasn't loud, it was easy to hold a conversation. He asked some really good, nonintrusive questions that we all answered honestly, as his inquisitiveness didn't pose a threat. He blended in well amongst our group, talking as if this wasn't our first-time meeting. We didn't think it was too strange, as most of the people there were married couples and a few other awkward single guys. Unfortunately, he became too comfortable, as what happened next is something we laugh and joke about to this day, and his reaction revealed so much about him.

By this time, Rob, as he introduced himself, had found his way back to our group after leaving a few times. I mean, how could he help it? Kenisha, Niya, and I were not only beautiful women, but we also loved to have fun and have good conversations. "I got you all figured out," Rob said confidently. "Really!?!" we exclaimed, confused. "Yeah, I do!" he replied, then sipped his drink. And within a split second, Niya open hand chopped him in the throat, causing Rob to spit out his recently sipped drink, clutching his throat, coughing and gasping for air while trying not to spill too much of the darkly colored spirit in his other hand. Kenisha and I were in sheer disbelief, as if someone had offered us a million dollars with no strings attached.

With wide eyes, confused faces, and open hands, we both screamed, "Niya!" demanding an explanation for her action. She so innocently and playfully replied, "What? Since he had us figured out, he should've seen that coming." Kenisha and I couldn't help but laugh, as we genuinely understood that though her actions were inappropriate, she had a point. And I know how weird this sounds, but we also knew that she truly meant no harm and had a unique way of bonding with people.

Poor Rob waved us off, still attempting to recover and process how he was assaulted by the "Cool Bmore Girls." How embarrassing? I was the guest who brought a guest who assaulted another guest. While Kenisha continued to interrogate Niya, I quickly went to attend to the watery-eyed, hunched-over Rob. Shaking my head and laughing, yet truly remorseful about my friend's actions, I said, "I am so sorry. Are you okay? Please forgive her." So many thoughts were running through my head, not knowing what type of guy he was. Would he want to retaliate by hitting her? Would he want to curse her out? Would he rally his female siblings or friends to meet her outside? Being from Baltimore, I had seen all of these scenarios unfold before.

Well, even though she was dead wrong, whatever the repercussions were, I was going to be right there, heels off, squared up. "What is wrong with her?" were the first words I clearly heard come out of his mouth. This time, no longer laughing, as I was still trying to figure him out, I said, "I am sooooo sorry. Are you okay? Is there anything I can get you?"

"Nahh, I'm good," he replied, still rightfully annoyed. "But seriously, what's wrong with her?" he demanded. All I could come up with was, "Niya is Niya. You have to get to know her to understand her. It was probably all the gin and tonics, but it wasn't meant to truly cause harm. She's really not that type of friend. She truly loves hard but plays a bit hard too at times," I said reassuringly.

Niya joined us, saying, "My bad. I didn't realize my karate skills were going to come forward like that." We all sort of chuckled, as she is noticeably African American mixed with Asian. Her playful grin and lighthearted demeanor seemed to diffuse some of the tension. I'm proud to say no one else had to be subject to Niya's throat chops, but not so proud that Rob received a second one from her later that evening. This time, it was a lot less violent. He thought it'd be best if he distanced himself from us but obviously was a glutton for punishment, as he found himself right back around us. Before the end of the evening, she did sincerely apologize, and he seemed to have forgiven her.

The moment we got in the car and started our hour drive from DC back to Baltimore, we all agreed that he was a nice guy and really cute. We also agreed that Niya can never assault a person like that again, as it could have been a bad situation for us all. We truly had a good time and replayed the night's festivities while we headed back home. As far as we knew, that encounter ended there.

A week later, after being tagged in a photo by April on social media, I received a friend request from a guy. I was very particular about who I let follow me. Clicking on his picture and navigating to his profile, I explored it more closely. "Wait, this is the guy that Niya chopped in the throat!" I immediately accepted it, went to the DM, and started to send little ninja bunny rabbit emojis, followed by the big, yellow-faced emoji that was choking. It had enlarged balloon cheeks and tears coming out of its squinted eyes. This was my way of ensuring that this was truly him.

"Oh, you got jokes?" he responded.

My response was about 25 crying laughing emojis. Of course, I couldn't help but have him painfully relive that night, as that was the only thing we had in common at that point. "I must admit, the way you handled that situation was pretty impressive," I typed, hoping he would feel the sincerity and see past all the jokes. "I've seen males hit females for less, and the way you were able to recover really stood out. You don't look like the pushover type."

He responded, "I deal with what most people would consider 'crazy people' every day."

He had me intrigued. The DM chats turned into conversations I looked forward to as they were very different. They weren't about surface things like my appearance or the typical "Why are you single?" questions. If a question started off as common, like "What do you do for a living?" it always went about six more layers deep. As the conversation was friendly, and I was on my "new me" campaign, it never dawned on me to ask about his relationship status. I didn't feel it was necessary as our chats felt purely platonic. Me "friend-zoning" a man was common, but for him not to try his hand? My curiosity took over. What was his angle? There's no way he can be this good of a dude! So, I did some unintentional recon.

Khary called my cell. "Geezie," which is what he still calls me to this day. "Hey there, King!" I replied.

"Well, I'm just getting around to calling everyone to thank them for helping April and me celebrate. It really meant a lot!" Khary is the type that really values quality time, true friendship and family over everything else. So, receiving this heartfelt call made complete sense.

"It was my pleasure. We had a great time. Thanks again for letting me invite my friends." That last part was strategic, just to see if Rob had told the guests of honor that one of their guests had assaulted him.

"No problem!" he replied. "Plus, you shut the party down, and you had a few brothas asking about you."

"Really?" I asked, my interest piqued.

After giving me the scoop, I wanted to confirm my suspicions about a guy I had been networking with at the party because his ulterior motives were questionable. Suspicion—intuition confirmed.

Previously, I scrolled lightly on Rob's social media, but nothing alarming stood out. I saw some pics of what appeared to be him with his kids and a few photos of what looked like his parents and siblings. I refused to do a deep dive because our conversations didn't move me to do that.

"Well, what's up with the guy, Rob?" I asked.

"Ooohhh, Rob!?" Khary responded. "Good brotha. Good dude. He's like my brotha from anotha muva."

"Yeah, Rob, soo uhhh…" He hesitated, and I could sense there was something behind his response that he felt conflicted about sharing.

"Well, Rob…" As I sat there patiently waiting, I wasn't really feeling any type of way because, at this point, there wasn't any noticeable chemistry but a genuine interest in the mystery behind "The guy that Niya chopped in the throat." He was very handsome and, from the chats (never speaking over the phone or using voice messages), seemed to be very intelligent, funny, and an all-around good person.

Khary paused before continuing, "So, yeah, Rob. He kinda has this situation where me and AJ, as he often referred to April, are hoping that they can work it out. He's married, and they have been having troubles for a while now."

Genuinely responding, "Oh, okay. I don't know the ends and outs of their situation, but I hope they do, too. I truly desire to see families stay together." I nodded, absorbing the information. It explained a lot about his deep, engaging conversations and why he hadn't made any moves. It also made me more guarded towards the man who handled a throat chop with such grace and humor.

From that point on, I didn't respond right away like before or even prompt the conversation. He kept communicating through chat as usual; unbeknownst to him, I had new information that he hadn't previously shared. Out of all fairness, it had only been a little over two weeks and about four or so deep conversations.

But nothing we'd discussed would've called for a need to share that information. If neither of us shared any romantic interest, bringing up "I'm married" would've alluded to one of us desiring more. Of course, that's how I rationalized it. To me, having this new information was the big joker, and it would only be played at the r ight time.

A few days later, after the formalities had been covered, he mentioned that he was cooking dinner. "Really? What are you cooking?" I asked. With this particular social media platform, when someone was typing a message, three dots within a bubble would jump as if three piano keys were being consecutively played over and over. After about three or so minutes of me looking at the screen, waiting for him to share what he had prepared because I had some follow-up questions, the bubbles continued to jump. He must've fallen asleep, or maybe there's a bad internet connection, I thought. Oh well.

Curious as to whether or not he had responded, about five minutes later, I opened the app, and bubbles were still jumping. "He must've burned whatever he's cooking and needs to give that his undivided attention," I thought. I decided to close the app out and give something else my attention. About 10 minutes after that, "ding," there was a notification that someone had sent me a message. As I saw the indicator flashing green, I assumed he had finally had the time to respond. When I opened the app, I was not expecting that!

He had typed a very long message—so long that it took me swiping from the bottom up at least five times before getting to the end of his message. What is this? I thought. As I scrolled back to the top and began to read, he shared the ages and genders of his children, the custody arrangement with his oldest son—that he fought for joint legal and physical custody because he didn't want to be a "part-time or weekend dad."

He shared that he was going through a separation, where he had been sleeping between the basement and guest room for quite some time. He shared how she wasn't a bad person, and he felt like they had tried everything. He also expressed his prolonged torment of finally coming to terms with the decision. Rob also expressed that he hadn't physically left because he wanted his children to be in a functioning household as long as possible, and he didn't want to leave her with figuring out the sale and all of the responsibilities that come with it on her own. He concluded this comprehensive dissertation with, "...and on top of that, she is five months pregnant." Reading his words, I realized how complex and painful his situation was

As I processed his message, I weighed my empathy for his situation against my commitment to avoid drama. It was a delicate balance. My first thought was that my heart truly goes out to her, as I am a woman and a mother. Pregnancy in itself is hard. But being pregnant and going through a separation, especially when you aren't the one who prompted it, I can't imagine. My second thought was this is a lot to digest, but I know he is on the other end wondering what I am thinking. Should I not respond, as I don't do drama, and this is pretty heavy? Well, that's not fair because if anyone can resonate with what he could be experiencing, it's me.

I took into account that I had people judging me based on my decision to get a divorce. I took into account that people who I thought had my back took the stance of stabbing it or remaining neutral. I thought about how I wished I had more friends who had actually been through it and could relate. But I had no one who could. I had those who really did their best and were there for me as much as they could be, like my cousin Tynisha, but she too had been limited by experience. So, after about 10 minutes of reading, 5 minutes of rereading, and 10 minutes of processing, I figured I'd respond with, "So, did you cook spaghetti?" In attempts to break the ice because what he unloaded on me was an iceberg.

That couldn't have been easy. But what that did show me, was that he was a man of integrity, and he had a conscience, and his unfortunate situation and circumstance was not who he was. How dare I judge him? We all go through moments in life that we aren't the proudest of and wish they had turned out another way. And those moments have their place in our human experiences. They are the added sugar or the omitted cocoa powder that wasn't meant to deter, define, or destroy us—it was meant to develop us. And this moment was oh too familiar to me

.

After several conversations of quizzing him on what they'd done to try and make it work, he said, "I've been gone, but I am physically here." I knew exactly what he meant. When in a hopeless relationship, you mentally, spiritually, and emotionally leave long before you physically do. I admired that I never heard him say anything bad or damaging about her. He'd say, "We just aren't right for one another." He continued, "I'm not looking for a relationship, and even if I never find one, I can't stay in this as it's not fair to anyone." I honestly believed him, as his actions matched his words thus far. But this was heavy!

Having this iceberg unloaded on me definitely had me frozen. Even though I hadn't previously considered it, this was confirmation that nothing more would ever develop, considering his unfortunate circumstances. The boundaries were set.

We kept in touch through DM and never even spoke on the phone until a couple of months later.

Why was I so open to befriending him? What happened to the woman code? Am I wrong? Are my intentions misguided? Would I want the same thing done to me? These were just a few of the million and one questions I asked myself. The confident, subtle, but reassuring words were, "I've been gone…" The truth is his character rose above the gravity of his circumstances—and that's what lured me in.

During the process of his youngest son being born and his divorce, it was a very uncharted time for me. At any moment, he could decide, "I changed my mind; I want to make it work." Though I was learning how to navigate this overly complicated and sensitive situation that had so many hearts involved, I was also learning what we could possibly look like together. More importantly, I was learning even more about myself.

I had to learn how to trust and unlearn how to shield my heart from anticipated hurt and understand that vulnerability is not a weakness. This was definitely a challenge for me. At this point, as far as I knew, he had been forthcoming about everything that had been taking place and provided proof, when possible, to substantiate his claims without me asking for it. I don't think he understood how much this was needed, as a past experience had left me wary of deceit.

There was a situation that "didn't count," where this guy I was seeing for a short—very short—period of time, the time between the exe's, that I found out he was "married-married". You know, the type where there were no talks of separation or divorce. The type where he was living a whole double life outside of her. Of course, once I found out (at this point, it was a confirmation), I threatened to "blow up the spot" if he ever tried to contact me again. However, the source of the confirmation assured me that his wife, though not in agreement, wouldn't be surprised. So, I decided to unsubscribe from whatever marriage edition they had goi ng on.

So, Rob's tactics and strategy—or maybe it was just him being considerate—were slowly working on me, helping me to work on myself.

The first part of our relationship was a fast-paced lane into a rollercoaster ride. We had moments where things were moving along, then moments of uncontrollable waiting. We had some uphill trudging, super highs, and breathtaking moments, followed by some stomach-knot balling, sweaty palms, twists, turns, and drops. He dealt with my disgruntled ex, and I dealt with being invited to a scene where the other cast members weren't aware of a new leading lady.

I had to learn how to communicate openly and unlearn the habit of bottling up my emotions. I had to learn how to be patient with his process and unlearn the tendency to rush through uncomfortable situations. I had to learn how to support someone going through a difficult time and unlearn the instinct to distance myself from pain. Because of the ugliness of this situation, he could've at any moment just stepped on it, disregarding the gook that it would leave. Why couldn't I have just met him at another point in life without this delicate, complicated storyline?

Despite the rollercoaster, these challenges were stripping me and clothing me, all in preparation for the next phase of our relationship. On the surface, it seemed ugly, slow, and underdeveloped, but it was purposeful, helping me gain the knowledge I needed and shed the things that no longer served me. It was a time of transformation and growth, where his character overshadowed his circumstances and showed me the value of perseverance and integrity.

This phase of my relationship with Rob mirrored a lesson I was beginning to learn in every aspect of my life: **Transformation often begins in the messiest, most uncomfortable places.** Just as our relationship required patience and perseverance, so, too, did my professional journey.

In the same way, I had to unlearn habits and embrace uncomfortable growth in my personal life. I found myself facing similar challenges in entrepreneurship. Starting a business, much like nurturing a new relationship, required me to confront fears, adapt to setbacks, and trust the process—even when the outcome wasn't clear.

Hungry for More

Entrepreneurship

In 2010, amidst the chaos of my separation and divorce, I experienced a profound awakening—a moment of revival. God charged me with a monumental task birthed from a life-changing revelation. This revelation exposed a crucial concept: the difference between a temporary mistake and an irrecoverable failure. It highlighted the blurred threshold that separates triumph from surrender, the fine line between love and hate. This overlooked, underrated cheat code to a happier life was...acceptance. Not just any acceptance but the deep, transformative power of self-acceptance. Acceptance of what was and the surrender of control over what will be. This revelation reshaped my journey, colorfully lighting the path to true peace and fulfillment.

The moment I came to terms with the part that I've played in this drama and what I vowed to do differently, not from a vengeful place, but from an aware place, my future looked brighter. When I looked back, in retrospect, I realized that I didn't love myself how I should've; otherwise, that marriage, that relationship, wouldn't have been acceptable. Now, I get it. It was me. I expected someone else to love me the way that I didn't even love myself. And now, the task was to help other women tap into the root of their "reality."

I started a women's organization called YANA (You Are Not Alone) that focused on helping women intentionally love themselves first so that they could not only be their best version for everyone else but, first and foremost, for themselves.

I chose that name because, at my lowest point, I heard God's sweet whisper say, "You Are Not Alone." That voice was so comforting yet so convicting that it pulled me out of a dark space. From that, I mustered up the courage, while still sleeping on my sister's couches and floors, to cultivate a space where other women who felt like they were doing life alone could come together and work on themselves, guilt-free. Initially, I was embarrassed when going through the toils of life, but I knew there were others like me. *The best way to get rid of the shame was to expose it to the light* so others could gleam hope from this newly developing picture.

It didn't matter that their lenses were different; the development of their unique angles, focus, and compositions would break the chains of embarrassment and pride, allowing them to find the sisterhood, serenity, and strategies needed to achieve their once-lustrous but forgotten goals. I wanted them to know it wasn't too late to create a masterpiece. I wasn't the only one who had a similar vision.

My cousin, best friend, sister, and the other side of my brain—we always balance each other out. Sometimes, I'm right, and she's left, and vice versa. Tynisha started a group called FLY (First Love Yourself) with a small group of her single friends who had a similar mission. We decided to merge the two groups; thus, YANA FLY was born. Our very first meeting had 22 women crammed in my sister's living room.

A few months after a couple of meetings, she realized that her passion was to support young and teenage girls (which she is still proudly doing to this day), so I carried the torch as I was locked in on what I had been charged to do.

For three years, with around 50 women later, we gathered monthly to dive into the essentials of self-awareness, self-forgiveness, self-correction, self-love, and self-commitment. It was during these gatherings that the 5 stages of The FLY Life Cycle came to life—a framework I created to make First Loving Yourself more practical and less like some far-off idea. Organizing our conversations through this cycle gave us a way to simplify what could feel overwhelming. It helped the women not just grasp the concepts but actually use them in real life, no matter where they were in their own growth process.

It was important to maintain healthy levels of self-acceptance while self-improving. We covered topics such as vision boarding, credit repair, saving, budgeting, couponing, meditation, health and wellness, relationships, boundary setting, and just "letting it out," and quarterly outings of "just getting out." We even participated in community give-back events where we got our children involved to help them stay connected to the world outside of themselves.

The lives I had the privilege to impact through this group were incredibly rewarding. But as the saying goes, all good things must come to an end. My purpose had shifted, and I felt released to let go of the group's formal structure. To this day, I remain connected with many of the women, and our shared journey continues to inspire me. However, it was time for me to shift my focus inward—to prioritize my own growth and revival. I needed to step boldly into the lessons I had been teaching and learning, showing through action what transformation truly looks like. I asked my daughters to bear with me during this very difficult time. I told them that they would see upgrades every two years, and I kept them abreast of the process and progress along the way.

The plan was simple in theory but daunting in execution: Phase 1—get a job, get a car, get a place. It was no easy task, but a year and a half later—done, done, and done! With Phase 1 complete, it was time to move on to Phase 2: get a better-paying job. The goal was to afford something better than "Big Baby," my black 2004 Dodge Durango, which spent more time at the mechanic's than on the road, and to upgrade from the two-bedroom apartment I barely tolerated. Between the roach infestations and the occasional smell of mice dying in the walls—thanks to the less-than-sanitary neighbors across the hall—I clearly needed a fresh start. To make all that happen, I had to go where the money was.

I decided it was time to continue pursuing the IT career I had been doing the Walz with since 1998. Yes, I took the bait—the beautifully written acceptance letter from The College of Notre Dame of Maryland (CND) lured me in. It was a small, predominantly white, all-girls Catholic College located on the east side of Baltimore. I was also offered a full-ride to Gettysburg College in Pennsylvania, which I cheerfully declined. I decided to attend CND instead due to the convenient location—ok, you saw through the smoke screen—it was because I was terrified and had not been prepared to be so far away from home on my own.

Gettysburg, though they too were only 4% black, did their best to be welcoming as they invited me to the college to experience the culture. During my visit there in 1997, I stayed overnight with a family, then took a week-long trip with 11 other college students and two adult chaperones to Georgia with the Quaker's organization to visit some historical sites, MLK Jr.'s burial site, museum, and the historical bridge.

We ended the trip in Tuskegee, Alabama, where we were a part of rebuilding two black churches that were burnt down due to hate crimes. I was the only black student and a high schooler. At the end of each night, we'd discuss our opinions and feelings based on what we'd learned and seen. They were constantly apologizing for what "their people" did to us. "I'm not the token black girl," I thought. They had no idea. That was a lot for me to process.

You would think that, with the sincere efforts of the staff, students, and college to show me that they were inclusive and open-minded to have more blacks attend their institution, I would've chosen to go there, right? To a 17-year-old, my brain didn't process it like that.

If anything happened, at least I could be home within 20 to 30 minutes, I thought to myself. So, I chose CND. My second semester, I got pregnant with my first-born, Tamir. Finishing college was the last thing on my mind; the first, was how would I tell my mother, take care of me and a child, all at 19. From 2000 until 2008, I took an IT certification program, participated in IT internships, and took all the classes I needed to get my bachelor's degree. Except, I didn't complete my Capstone project.

Midway through, I gave up. I failed. It had simply gotten too hard. I was juggling the emotional strain of trying to inject understanding into an unfulfilling marriage, welcoming my daughters, Ta'Qara and Ta'Rheeyn, into the family, and navigating the fallout of the housing market crisis—all while working as a Title Processor in the real estate industry. On top of that, a 264-page project with intricate networking diagrams and infrastructure, plus a presentation portion, wasn't exactly a priority.

With only two classes left to finish, I walked away. One of them was an irrelevant class they made you take just to tack on more fees—kind of like those exit interviews that feel more like hoops to jump through than anything meaningful.

Honestly, I wish I had known then what I know now. I wouldn't have racked up six-figures in student loan debt achieving a degree for an industry that technically doesn't require it for what I wanted to do. Industry certifications would've been cheaper, quicker, and more effective in achieving that goal.

Now 2013, as the livelihood of my daughters and I depended on it, not only did I get A's in my last two courses, but I proudly walked across the stage receiving my Bachelor's in Information Systems. Less than a year later, I got a promising job in networking and telecommunications making 65k and amazing benefits! That salary allowed me to swiftly accomplish phase 2.

Now on to Phase 3. Can you guess what it was? Rinse and repeat—this time with bigger goals. I was ready to pursue that six-figure salary. I wanted a larger, better home, as my oldest daughter needed more privacy from her younger sisters, who were 5 and 7 years younger. A new vehicle wasn't a priority as long as the one I had was trustworthy but saving money had become a top priority.

While still grinding in Phase 2, I developed a framework I called the KNC Stack Theory: stack your knowledge, stack your network, and stack your coins. This method was so effective it allowed me to accomplish Phase 3 in less than two years—and I even wrote an e-book about it to help others accelerate their growth while navigating a 9-to-5. Using this framework, I earned highly sought-after IT certifications—for free, connected with people who could put my name in rooms

I might never step foot in, and fully leveraged benefits packages to save money and secure free financial perks.

Phase 3 was my ultimate goal. I believed reaching it would bring the "perfect life." I had the career I'd worked so hard for, the kind of man I'd prayed for, and the life I'd promised my daughters. I'd landed a role at a top global IT company, where, once again, I was the only Black woman in the room.

I traveled all over for work, experiencing new things all the time on the company's dime. I spoke in rooms in front of hundreds of people, yet I was missing something. My supervisor would ask me what my next steps were, but I never had an answer; I just knew that this wasn't going to be it. All that planning and achieving goals still didn't provide me with that perfect life I longed for.

Have you noticed that some of us are on vicious cycles of setting and accomplishing goals, with the hopes that each new goal we accomplish is going to be the one that fills that void we are missing? Just one more promotion, one more raise, this car, that house, this degree, that relationship, this weight, or that opportunity. Why is that? *This relentless pursuit of external validation can leave us feeling even emptier as we overlook the true source of fulfillment—inner alignment and purpose.*

Thanks to God's grace and the unwavering encouragement and support of my king and daughters, I made a bold decision: I was going to start my own life coaching business. Yes, I chose to walk away from it all. At the time, I had no idea what it truly meant to run—or even start—a life coaching business. All I knew was that I was seeking fulfillment, and I needed to break free from the vicious cycle I had been trapped in. To step into this new chapter, I had to let go of some things to learn some things.

I had to divorce my idea of what success and happiness looked like and marry the plan that God had for me. That plan had been there all along, waiting for me to recognize it. What wasn't there, however, was the mindset I needed to transition from the structured, "stable," and "sustainable" 9-to-5 life to the unpredictable world of being self-employed. It was a leap of faith—equal parts exciting and nerve-wracking—but I knew it was the step I had to take to align with my true purpose.

One thing that I've come to learn about God's plans for our lives is that He rarely reveals too much at once—at least, that's been my experience. I believe this is intentional and deeply strategic. If He laid out the entire step-by-step plan from the beginning, would we still feel the need to seek Him, consult Him, or talk to Him regularly? Probably not. Our relationship with Him would become transactional instead of transcendent.

God wants us to cast all our cares on Him, not just so He can provide for us, but so our relationship with Him can be strengthened. Psalm 37:5 (ESV) reminds us, " *Commit your way to the Lord; trust in him, and he will act.*" Trusting Him becomes easier when we reflect on how He's provided for us in the past.

How are relationships strengthened? Through trust—trust that the other person will follow through on what they've said and that their actions are guided by what's best for you. With God, this trust is built step by step as we lean on Him and witness His faithfulness unfold.

Secondly, God doesn't reveal too much upfront because let's face it, we are bound to mess something up. Since the beginning of time, we've somehow convinced ourselves that we've got it all figured out, operating with our finite wisdom. I can think of countless times when I faced calamity simply because I thought I knew better. I either didn't consult God or outright disobeyed Him. What's more, in most of those situations, I knew deep down that what I was pursuing wasn't what He had for me.

Some might call it intuition, but for me, these moments go much deeper and they're honestly much clearer than that.

The third reason, and perhaps one of the most profound, is that He wants the glory. At first glance, that might sound conceited, but think about it this way: Have you ever been a major part of someone's life, helping and guiding them along the way, only to watch them achieve something without your input? Sure, you might be happy for them, but deep down, you may have felt a twinge of questioning, "Do they even need me anymore?" It's natural to want to feel needed and valued, especially when you've been pivotal to someone's success.

God desires the same, but on a much greater scale. He wants to remain the head of your life. Consulting Him with your decisions demonstrates reverence, trust, and humility. It's a declaration that you recognize you can't do it without Him. For those of us who are parents—or who play a parental role—it's easier to grasp this concept. We love it when our children turn to us, not just out of necessity but because they value our wisdom and guidance. Our Heavenly Father desires the same. His plan is paramount, and He longs for us to put Him first so He can be glorified in every step of our journey.

This desire for God to be at the center of our lives extends beyond spiritual matters; it influences every aspect of our journey, including our careers and personal aspirations. With entrepreneurship, the process of starting a business can feel much like a leap of faith. It's an endless crawl marked by slow progress and countless challenges. It's easy to get frustrated when success doesn't come as quickly as we'd hoped, but these early struggles are essential for building a strong foundation.

For me, deciding to start a life coaching business was the easy part. The interesting—and far more challenging—part was learning how to run one. In many ways, the process reminded me of the caterpillar's crawl: a slow, deliberate journey driven by a hunger for growth and a vision for something greater. And just as the caterpillar's crawl extends beyond a single branch, my own struggles weren't confined to my business. They mirrored a deeper area of transformation in my life—my health. Both demanded patience, persistence, and the courage to confront deeply rooted beliefs about what I thought was "normal."

The Weight of It All

Health

hy are we so desensitized to some of the signals that our bodies send us when something is not right? "Oh, that's just the way it is," we say. I'm not saying we should be hypochondriacs, over-dramatizing every ache and pain, but the way we ignore blatant signs of discomfort seems almost inhumane.

While experiencing a heavy cycle, the women in my family didn't speak to the abnormalities of it. Probably because they didn't know it was abnormal and because catering to aches and pains is not at the forefront of their minds. More "important" things exist there, like making ends meet, taking care of family, and the other hundreds of responsibilities and tasks assigned to them. As if my heavy cycles and paralyzing cramps, nausea, and headaches weren't enough, once I had my first child at 19, things worsened.

I would burn through a pack of 36 long, thick pads during my 7-day cycle, and that's not even counting the spotting that dragged on for days before and after. Let's talk about the woman with the issue of blood. I remember the countless times I had to change my clothes after embarrassing accidents—throwing away stained sheets and panties because no amount of soaking or scrubbing could fully remove the crimson evidence. TMI (too much information)? Perhaps, but it's important for you to understand the years of silent struggle. I know some of you can feel my pain. And speaking of pain...

Not only were my cycles violently crimson, but they were excruciatingly painful—relentless. I'd find myself curled up in bed, knees pulled tight to my chest, arms gripping my legs like a lifeline. My chin rested on my kneecaps, my eyes squeezed shut, and my jaw clenched to the point of aching as I tried to suppress the groans. The pain wasn't just sharp—it spread like wildfire from my core, shooting out in both directions and leaving me breathless with each wave.

If you've not had to experience it, that's wonderful, as I wouldn't wish any of it on my worst enemy. Considering how much I was reminded, "You are a child, and I am an adult, and you need to stay in a child's place, surely someone—some adult had the answers to cure me of this seemingly never-ending cycle of agony.

My mom's remedy was always the same: "That's why you need to stop walking around barefoot." I couldn't quite grasp the correlation or rationale. "Which one came first—menstrual cycles and cramps or shoes?" I wondered silently, of course. I wasn't bold enough to find out if her hand or the nearest object would reach me first.

The funny thing is, even though we'd moved up North, I was born down South, and the country life was in my blood. Back then, running around barefoot wasn't just a choice; it was a way of life. It felt so freeing to feel the cold mud between my toes, the dew-soaked grass blades under my feet, or the compacted, dusty dirt roads beneath my soles. And yes, this is coming from the same little girl who loved to change clothes at least five times a day. But that's why I did it—being present, immersed in nature. Even if I didn't fully understand why at the time, it just felt ri ght.

So, why my mom thought the presence of shoes would be the cure for my menstrual misery was beyond me. Well, since the women in my family didn't have the answers, I figured it was time to consult someone who might.

With her heavy Indian accent, "This is normal for young ladies your age," the doctor said, all matter-of-factly. "I'm going to prescribe a low dose of birth control pills, and you can get some iron supplements over the counter. Let's see how that works for the next 90 days. But I'm confident that should do it!" Her solution? To put me on drugs. Drugs?!?! Drugs??? *Drugs!!!!*

FINALLY! Someone with an answer to this life of torment! This little ole Indian woman with the sweetest disposition delivered the answer straight from Heaven's gates, and I touched the hem of her lab coat, believing I'd finally found healing. But unlike the miraculous moment where Jesus felt virtue leave His body and declared, "Your faith has made you well," there was no immediate relief. No instantaneous cure. Just a piece of paper with a prescription I didn't fully understand and a sense of hope that maybe, just maybe, this would be my "go and be made whole" moment.

But where was my healing touch? Where was my miraculous turnaround? No voice from Heaven, no sudden end to my suffering. Instead, I was left with a starter pack of pills—camouflage-colored like those little rounded pink pocket mirrors we used to carry around in the early '90s and a regimen, waiting for some hint of normalcy. Maybe my faith would be in the tiny white tablets instead of a divine encounter. I mean, I'd heard stories of Jesus laying hands and the blind seeing, the crippled walking, and demons being cast out. I couldn't help but think: Surely, if He could do all that, a little crimson tide would be light work for Him, right?

Yet, here I was, walking out of that office, clutching a prescription and trying to reconcile modern medicine with the miracles of the Bible. "Did I just trade the hem of the garment for the healthcare system?" I thought, shuddering at the irony. But hey, if He used mud and spit to heal a blind man, maybe He could work through these pills, too. I figured I'd do what the woman with the issue of blood did: hold on to faith and wait for the day my bleeding, at minimum, the cramps, would stop.

That brief moment of jubilee was interrupted by a nagging thought: *Why am I only now being prescribed birth control pills after going through 10,000 pads, 5,000 tampons, 50 bedspreads, and 100 pairs of panties? Not to mention one whole little human later!* I guess the complaints of extreme fatigue and pain weren't enough of a clue that something more needed to be done.

Then, it hit me like a ton of bricks. The church's strict stance against young girls being on birth control had conditioned my mom to rule it out entirely, missing the possibility that it could have offered some much-needed relief. It seemed easy to place the blame on her shoulders. But as I grew older, I realized she was only doing the best she could with the limited information she had, battling the weight of external judgment and internal conflict all at once. That's when I understood the full complexity of our struggle—one that wasn't just physical but also cultural, emotional, and deeply rooted in faith.

Through these experiences, I've learned that transformation doesn't always start with visible change; sometimes, it begins quietly—within the confines of discomfort, cultural beliefs, and personal limitations. This process isn't immediate, and it's not always beautiful. It's a slow shedding of old patterns, a voracious consumption of new truths, and an awkward growth into something different. Something stronger.

Each journey had its share of uncomfortable, awkward, and seemingly unproductive moments. Yet, it's precisely these stages that shaped me into who I am today. They were more than just painful detours; they were necessary intervals of growth that prepared me for the transformation to come.

Each of these experiences underscored an essential truth: ***transformation often begins quietly, hidden within the discomfort and limitations we face.*** These seemingly unproductive moments are not wasted—they are deliberate intervals that shape us into something stronger, something new.

Growing on Purpose

Patient Perspective

J ust as my relationship, entrepreneurship, and health journeys began with unexpected challenges, nature offers us parallels that teach us about patience and deliberate growth. Let's take a look into the larva stage from a *patient perspective, which characteristics are: unique, deliberate, fascinating, independent, transformative, purposeful, and developing.* Did you know that "larva" refers to an early form of any animal that, at birth or hatching, is very different from its parents and undergoes a complete metamorphosis—not just butterflies? Think of frogs, grasshoppers, crickets, and beetles, just to name a few. I can almost hear you say, *"None of them end up pretty."* I know, but that's not the point.

Often, we internalize our "ugly stage" as if we're the only ones experiencing it. I share this to help you see this phase as a universal experience rather than a personal or individual attack. Your "ugly stage" isn't a punishment; it's purposeful. Its uniqueness lies in how it develops you uniquely.

Consider the journey of a caterpillar. Its primary purpose during the larva stage is to eat and grow, consuming large amounts of food to fuel rapid development. Caterpillars—like many larvae—feed on plant leaves and other vegetation, shedding their skin each time they grow. This ravenous consumption allows them to quickly increase in size and mass, preparing for the next stage in their life cycle.

Don't quite see the connection? Our lives mimic this pattern of consuming, growing, and shedding. Think about it. The challenge isn't consumption itself but rather developing a harmonious rhythm or balance among all three.

Most people are natural consumers. Having our five senses—sight, smell, touch, taste, and hearing—makes us easily susceptible to taking in information and experiences, whether we're aware of it or not. On social media, we see someone enjoying a beautiful vacation with azure waters and clear, sunny skies, and suddenly, we wish we were there too. We walk past a bakery, smell the aroma of freshly baked bread, and now we crave it. We hear someone's negative opinion about another person, and without realizing it, we start forming our own biases.

Consumption doesn't rely on whether we actually obtain the things we desire; it's about the information we ingest, which then affects our thoughts, feelings, and actions. Consuming isn't inherently "bad." In fact, it's crucial for survival. But some of us become habitual consumers, taking in things we never use productively.

Consumption is necessary for us to survive and thrive in this ever-evolving world. The real issue isn't consumption itself but rather our resistance to shedding what no longer serves us.

We cling to thoughts, habits, and behaviors that have long since expired their usefulness. We hold on to who we once were—the thinner, more ambitious, and driven version of ourselves—or maybe the carefree, more confident version. "What's wrong with wanting that?" you might ask. The problem is that we're fighting against the inevitable.

Each day we live, we age, even if we can't see it happening. And aging isn't something to fight against. It's not a "loss" or something to mourn—it's an ongoing transformation. It's a beautiful progression that signifies growth and wisdom. We must remember that growth sometimes means letting go of what once was to make room for what's yet to be.

Our bodies undergo various cycles of renewal, much like the phases of our lives. Different parts of us are constantly regenerating—consuming resources, growing, and shedding—just as we do emotionally and mentally. Consider the skin, which replaces its outer layer every 28 to 30 days in young adults, ensuring old cells give way to new, healthier ones. Or hair, which follows its own unique cycle of growth, rest, and shedding, ensuring that it's constantly renewed.

Even our nails are on their own schedule, regenerating more rapidly for fingernails compared to toenails. Ever noticed how quickly your nails bounce back after a small chip? Imagine if we could recover from setbacks in life with that same resilience and efficiency.

Our bones, though often thought of as permanent and unchanging once you pass puberty, are also engaged in a constant dance of breakdown and rebuilding—a powerful reminder that renewal happens even in the strongest parts of ourselves. Our eyelashes, blood cells, and even the tissues surrounding our teeth follow a similar process, all working together to ensure that old, damaged parts are replaced with something new.

This isn't just biology—it's a metaphor for growth. Just as our bodies let go of the old to make way for the new, we, too, must recognize what's no longer serving us and embrace the renewal process.

Proper nourishment—whether through food, thoughts, or experiences—ensures that this process unfolds smoothly, yielding more vibrant and fulfilling results. Imagine what would happen if, every few months, you deliberately evaluated what needed to be shed in your life—thoughts, habits, or even relationships that are stunting your growth. By choosing to let go, we create space for the new and thrive in our next phase.

Everyone wants to grow but often doesn't want to let go of the familiar. Holding onto dead things gives you a false sense of security, making you feel safe and stable, even though what you're clinging to no longer serves you. Would you try to glue back on your real lash that fell off or attempt to hold onto dead skin? I don't think so! Even if you temporarily patch up a broken nail, it's still not receiving nourishment like the rest because it's disconnected and severed from its source.

This entire caterpillar stage—from the first bite to the final shedding—is one of relentless growth, resilience, and preparation. In my relationship, this stage began with an unusual and uncomfortable truth: Rob was going through a divorce with his pregnant wife when we met. It was a weird situation to navigate, and it forced me to confront my own fears and rid myself of old insecurities. Yet, through his integrity and perseverance, he showed me I could trust him, even in the midst of chaos.

Entrepreneurship mirrored this same slow crawl. Starting a women's organization had been my first love and my inspiration for life coaching, but life's twists led me to a corporate job, only to be let go when I least expected it. The decision to start a life coaching business was the easier part—learning how to run it became the real challenge.

In health, I had to unlearn generations of normalized suffering, like believing heavy cycles were just part of life. Birth control seemed like a quick fix, but it didn't address the underlying issues that needed transformation. Across all these areas, progress wasn't immediate or glamorous—it was uncomfortable and awkward, filled with shedding old beliefs and consuming new truths.

While the caterpillar may lack the immediate allure of the butterfly, its role is undeniably fundamental. The transformations and groundwork during this stage lay the foundation for the beauty and grace of the adult butterfly. This stage teaches us that progress can be slow and not always immediately visible. Yet, without this period of deliberate growth, the final transformation simply wouldn't be possible.

The caterpillar's deliberate process prepares it to form a pupa or chrysalis, where it will then undergo its dramatic metamorphosis into a butterfly. Essentially, the caterpillar's primary job is to fuel its future transformation—to become a mature insect capable of reproduction, ensuring the continuation of its species' life cycle.

Often, we compare ourselves to the "butterfly," thinking we'd be better off skipping the caterpillar stage altogether. But if you reflect on your own life's caterpillar stages, you might realize those periods that feel slow, unattractive, and perhaps even repulsive are often when you're growing the most. Embrace these stages, recognizing that they are preparing you for your own magnificent transformation. Without this season of unseen growth, your most vibrant and capable self may never fully emerge.

Consuming | Growing | Shedding

Transformation Truths

A s we reflect on the lessons of the caterpillar stage, let's consider a few key truths that can help us navigate these slow, deliberate seasons of growth with purpose and patience. Are you ready to face the truth about the importance of growing through what you go through?

Deliberate Growth and Resilience: During the larva stage, we are in a state of deliberate growth. Caterpillars consume and shed, constantly preparing for the next phase. Think about times in your life when you felt like you were just "going through the motions." These periods are crucial for accumulating the resources and resilience needed for future transformations.

Transformative Eating and Shedding: Much like caterpillars eat and shed to grow, we, too, must consume knowledge and shed old habits. What are you consuming? Is it packed with nutritional value, or does it have tons of empty calories? An easy way to identify nutritional value is to gauge how quickly and consistently you are shedding things. Reflect on how you can feed your growth by learning new skills and letting go of what no longer serves you. Each shed skin is a step closer to your true potential.

Unique Challenges and Independence: Caterpillars face many challenges, yet they continue to grow independently. In our lives, we must navigate unique obstacles while maintaining our sense of independence. Recognize that these challenges are part of the process and build the strength needed for future stages.

Purposeful Preparation: The caterpillar stage is about purposeful preparation. Everything the caterpillar does is geared toward becoming a butterfly. Similarly, our efforts during challenging times are preparing us for greater things. Trust that your current struggles have a purpose and are setting the stage for your future success.

Patient Development: The larva stage teaches us the value of patient development. Just as the caterpillar grows slowly and steadily, we, too, must be patient with our progress. This patience involves actively engaging in self-improvement and maintaining a positive outlook, knowing that every step, no matter how small, contributes to our overall growth.

Reflection and Anticipation: Reflect on your own life and identify your larva stages. What areas are you currently identifying as ugly that you can now reframe as developing? How can you embrace this growth period with patience and purpose?

Practice the power of forethought. How could this stage possibly help you achieve your greater goal? Having a hard time with this concept? Focus more on proper consumption, whether it's physically, spiritually, mentally, emotionally, or all the other "llys" you can think of, and watch how growth starts to happen organically. "How will I know I am growing if I'm unable to see it?" Oftentimes, you can feel it. Take time to pay attention to how you are feeling around certain people, or places or when participating in certain activities. This could be an indication of misalignment.

Affirmation: *"I embrace the process of growth, knowing that each step is preparing me for transformation."*

A Butterfly's Transformation

"Before I crossed paths with Life Coach Von, I had no idea what my purpose was. I was hopping from job to job, chasing after promises of success, but not truly knowing what success was or, more importantly, what success meant to me. I was always seeking more money to fill a void I honestly didn't understand untilI started working with Coach Von. LifeCoach Von has helped me realize that true fulfillment lies in the journey of first loving yourself and purpose. Through her coaching, I learned to embrace patience as a virtue, understanding that the most meaningful transformation takes time. She helped me see that trusting the process is not about just waiting for things to happen but actively engaging in each moment with deliberate intention and faith.

Because of Life Coach Von, I no longer see success as a destination to be reached right away, but a journey. She has empowered me to trust in the unfolding of my own unique path, and for that, I am forever grateful."

~ Crystal Wilson AKA Money Coach Mo

Metamorphosis Moment

*The **caterpillar stage** reveals that growth requires both hunger and sacrifice. It teaches us that consuming the right knowledge and shedding the unnecessary prepares us to carry the weight of the transformation we're destined for.*

~ Life Coach Von

Chapter 6 The Chrysalis Stage

"You made all the delicate, inner parts of my body

and knit me together in my mother's womb.

Thank you for making me so wonderfully complex!

Your workmanship is marvelous—how well I know it.

You watched me as I was being formed in utter seclusion,

as I was woven together in the dark of the womb.

You saw me before I was born.

Every day of my life was recorded in your book.

Every moment was laid out

before a single day had passed.

How precious are your thoughts about me, O God.

They cannot be numbered!

I can't even count them;

they outnumber the grains of sand!

And when I wake up,

you are still with me!"

Psalm 139: 13-18 (NLT)

Stuck in the Dark

Impatient Perspective

Characteristics: *dormant,   stagnant,   dark,   uncertainty, questionable, unformed, secluded, a mess, identity-less, and trapped.*

"**N**ow, what do you think about the third stage, the chrysalis stage, often referred to as the cocoon stage?" Their shoulders shrugged, and their heads retracted as if retreating into a turtle shell. "It's such a dark and secluded stage," one said. Another added, "Honestly, I don't know what to think. I have no idea what's going on in there. All I know is, it goes in there as a caterpillar and comes out a butterfly," throwing their hands up in sheer confusion.

Mimicking being confined with clenched fists and a tense posture, another person said, "It feels like being trapped. There's no way out, no freedom. I can only imagine that it's a mess in there. I mean, I'm sure that some really interesting things have to happen for it to come out a butterfly. Then, on the other hand, maybe nothing's happening at all!" they continued, feeling perplexed and quite silly for not having a clear answer.

Much like the previous stage, there was not one positive perspective. Why do we immediately default to the negative unless the positive is apparent? Not one of them paused or chose to dig deep for a perspective that was different from their usual response. "Can you find one thing positive about it?" I asked. "Well, I do wish sometimes I could be alone too," one person said sarcastically. That wasn't the positive perspective that I was reaching for, though. Others boycotted the idea of looking for the bright side. I couldn't blame them.

How could they lay claim or connect with something they couldn't see? Who wants to be stagnant when we've been conditioned since birth that there's always more to have and go after? After taking one step, you need to take another and another to get somewhere. After Pre-K and kindergarten, there's first grade, and so on. After this job, you should be looking for a promotion.

Our culture and society don't support the idea of being stagnant unless you are recovering from something major. *Being in the pupa stage feels identity-less because it's a phase where the caterpillar is no longer what it was but also not yet what it's supposed to be.*

Truth be told, I understood where they were coming from. You must be a butterfly enthusiast to know what truly happens at this stage. I didn't initially know either, but life helped me to understand this stage more than a depiction or graph could tell. So, considering you may not be a butterfly enthusiast, let's temporarily set aside the connection of the butterfly and let's focus on the word stagnant—which most people identify this stage with and oftentimes their lives.

According to Merriam-Webster, stagnant means (1) not flowing in a current or stream and (2) without inflow and outflow or not advancing or developing. It's interesting because we, yes, me included, often use words that don't necessarily apply fully to our situation, and then we get discouraged because we have adopted the belief that this newly identified label is the truth. Then we get stuck there because we only use it at a surface level, but the subconscious impact is much deeper. Even with being a lover of definitions, I fall prey to this unhelpful and unhealthy habit.

If we take this definition and apply it accordingly, we should use it as an indicator. If we feel stagnant, that doesn't mean there is no movement; it may just mean that the movement doesn't appear to be progressive. So, instead of being discouraged by feeling stagnant, begin to acknowledge, accept, and take advantage of the temporary moment to get you flowing again. I know all too well how this feels as I've gotten plenty of practice in my relationship, business, and health.

Strength in the Stillness

Relationship

T hings moved quickly in our relationship as we—both individually and together—intentionally engaged in a lot of consuming, growing, and shedding. We didn't force things to happen; it just felt right whenever they did. It was as if a masterpiece was gradually being revealed. We couldn't get enough of each other's company, so it only made sense to begin integrating our families and introducing our kids to the picture. He was the first to meet my daughters, but not exactly by design.

After attending my birthday party, my daughters had quite a bit to say. My oldest daughter, along with my brother, was checking guests in at the door. "Your name?" my daughter asked, clipboard in hand.

"Robert Evans," he responded.

"Mom, that had to be the mystery man you've been seeing," she whispered to me later. Though I didn't always share the specifics of my comings and goings, I had been strategically transparent about certain things. Being a single mother, it wasn't just about keeping my daughters aware of my whereabouts; it was about establishing a different type of relationship with them—one rooted in trust and understanding.

No, not like girlfriends, but a bond that was trusting, transparent, and transformative. I would openly share lessons I'd learned in relationships and in life, hoping to create a safe space where they could feel comfortable being vulnerable with me. I wanted them to know it was okay to share their experiences without fear of judgment. In return, I made sure to model a bit of that vulnerability, too. To this day, I'm glad I did because it has only strengthened our connection.

So, when my daughter said, "That just had to be the mystery man you've been seeing," it wasn't out of line. But what struck me most was when she added, "There's just something about him. He looked like your type!"

Now, Rob definitely has his own style. At my party, he was dressed head-to-toe in a crisp white summer ensemble—light gray hat, white blazer, white cargo-style pants, and light gray high-top sneakers as the base. But in true Rob-esk fashion, he added his signature flair: a multicolored lavender, dark purple, and pink snakeskin-printed shirt and matching socks, subtly accented with hints of white and gray. I know it's hard to imagine, but you really just had to see him—calm, cool, and collected.

His facial hair was low and neatly trimmed, highlighting his smooth caramel skin with its warm red undertone. And those dimples—so deep and captivating, they were like charming little craters carved into his cheeks, drawing you in. His bright smile lit up the room, effortlessly becoming the main attraction.

And his scent? Masculine, yet subtle—noticeable enough to draw you in, making you want to linger in the space he left behind, just to savor the trace of his essence a little longer. Even if he simply walked by, you'd find yourself leaning into the down draft, hoping to capture that inviting, lingering fragrance one more time.

But how does a 14-year-old know my "type" when the only men she's ever seen me with were her father and one other serious relationship? Neither of whom looked anything like Rob or each other, for that matter. Maybe she was talking about the type that aligned with the "new me." The me that had been focused on being FLY—First Loving Yourself! That had to be it.

In true sisterly fashion, she promptly notified her sisters, giving them the full 411. They took one look at him and agreed that there was indeed something about him—they, too, saw him as "my type." Even though it was hard to admit it to them at the moment, they were definitely on to something, and it was reassuring to know they could see it, too.

My introduction to his children wasn't as accidental or playful as his introduction to mine. We both agreed that it needed to be handled with care, considering the sensitive nature of his recent divorce—just six short months ago. Now that I think about it, meeting on Valentine's Day doesn't sound all that strategic, does it? *Lol*. But at the time, our intentions were genuine. Given the shared physical and legal custody arrangement he fought so hard for, Rob was determined not to be a "weekend father."

"I refuse to be a weekend father," he told me once, his conviction clear. It was one of those moments that deepened the connection I had so quickly fallen into. Because of this arrangement, his kids were with him that day, and since it was our first Valentine's Day as a couple, we wanted to spend at least part of it together.

By this time, my daughters were already fond of him, and they were eager to meet his children. They imagined his kids would be a younger, even more fun extension of him. Given the sporadic and often non-existent support from my daughters' father, they were more than willing to be present and supportive that day.

So, we came up with a plan to spend the day together—playing games and sharing a meal in a neutral, nonintrusive setting. It felt like the best way for our two worlds to merge naturally.

His oldest son was 15, his daughter 4, and that last little surprise from his ex—the one he'd shared in his long, heartfelt message to me—was now a 6-month-old cute baby boy. The oldest didn't appear to have cared much. He had never experienced his mother and dad as a couple, and his relationship with Rob's ex was estranged from what I'd gathered. The other two were so young, even though his daughter was (and still is very intelligent), that I can gather they had no idea we were a couple, as we were sure not to lead on to that. Well, the first time should be the hardest, so they say (and we thought), and we had that one in the bag, and the second, fifth, and tenth... commingling was great!

We spent so much time together that the year seemed to fly by! There wasn't a single week that went by without us being together at some point. It was becoming ridiculous to maintain two separate households when we practically lived at one or the other's place. Neither place, however, was conducive to a family of eight. By now, it was clear where we were headed, so almost two years after meeting, we began to entertain the idea of purchasing a home together.

Wait, are you kidding me? Before marriage? Before an engagement or some sort of formal commitment? It seemed crazy at first, but there weren't many things I was certain of—except for him. If I were to take this step with anyone, it would be Robert. No other man in my life had ever been as consistent and made me and my daughters feel as safe and loved as he did.

Besides, we were just talking at that point and agreed it wouldn't be for at least another year. This timeframe would give him an opportunity to sort out lingering matters from his divorce, allow my oldest daughter to graduate high school (which was conveniently right across the street from the townhome I was renting), and give us time to start saving jointly. As the months passed, we talked more deliberately about what it would look like to blend our families into one household.

But then reality nudged us. His basement kept flooding, and my rent was increasing by $400 a month—along with a growing list of other inconveniences. One day, he suggested that we just start looking to see what was out there. We did not want to move immediately, but we wanted to get an idea of what our options were so we'd be prepared when the time came. Besides, it would take time to find the perfect home that could comfortably accommodate our blended family of eight.

We decided to enlist help from our sister from another mister, April, to check out some homes. After a few weeks, she sent us several listings. One in particular caught my eye. By this time, we'd already agreed on an area that would be suitable for us all and still maintain a decent proximity for him to manage his every-other-day arrangement with his children.

Though he encouraged me to go take a look at a house that just came on the market, I hesitated. "I mean, what do you have to lose?" he said casually. I knew he was right, but deep down, I sensed that neither of us was ready to admit that maybe, just maybe, we were more prepared for this step than we wanted to believe. "I guess you're right," I conceded and asked April to take me to see the house.

It checked nearly everything off our list—except it was a bit outdated, lacked a deck, and the school ratings didn't meet the standard I set for my daughters. But most of all, I didn't have *the moment*. Every place I've ever lived has always given me a vision, a literal snapshot that would capture me on the spot. It could be something small—a bathroom window, a unique sconce, the layout of the floor plan—something that spoke to me and made me say, *This is it. This is where I'm supposed to be.* But I felt none of that.

So much for that house! I shared my honest review with April and Rob. It wasn't what we wanted, but it gave me something even more valuable—a chance to visualize us there as a family. I found myself mapping out which child would get which room, imagining who would claim which corner for their things. I could see us having space to spread out instead of all eight of us cramming ourselves onto the cramped leather sectional in his tiny townhome living room. I pictured us gathered around the large kitchen island, chatting while we cooked together, instead of being cramped in my galley-style kitchen where we had to turn sideways just to let someone pass.

Looking back, I realize that Rob knew exactly what he was doing. By suggesting that I view homes, he opened a door for me to imagine, dream, and desire a home that truly fit us. He was planting seeds of possibility and stirring up anticipation. It allowed me to envision the life I wanted for my daughters and myself—a stable, welcoming environment—and, in turn, how I could help bring some stability and comfort to his children as well.

Sometimes, you need to sit in a space, touch it, or just be exposed to it without expectations or pressure. This act of being in proximity to your dreams allows them to seem more real and more achievable. I later learned through both life experiences and studying neuroscience that this is more than just wishful thinking—it's a powerful combination of science and spirit. Being exposed to what you desire, even passively, begins to align your thoughts and emotions with what could be, ultimately manifesting it into your reality.

This simple act stirred up excitement and gratitude within me. It helped me accept that not only could I provide the stable home environment I'd always prayed for, but I could also be part of mending some of the brokenness his kids might feel from their parents' separation. I had no intention of replacing their mother—I just wanted them to experience that even when life feels uncontrollable and uncertain, there's still so much beauty to be found in creating something new.

I could almost see us as our own modern-day African American Brady Bunch. But little did I forget, even they had their fair share of drama.

Just a few short days after visiting the house, April reached out to us on a shared group chat, exclaiming, "I found it!" Rob's immediate response was, "Tell them we want it!"

"What, without seeing it?" April protested.

"Well, Von just got back from a work trip, and I know she's exhausted. I'm available to go see it, but not sure when she will be."

I was groggily catching up on the texts as my phone kept vibrating incessantly with their back-and-forth messages. The notifications were blurring together as much as my post-nap vision. *What's all this commotion about?* I thought.

"This is a treasure," April insisted. "It has a walkout basement and everything. It's been on the market for six months, and they just dropped the price. There's no way it's going to stay much longer."

"I trust you, and you know what we're looking for," Rob replied with urgency. "Tell them we want it!"

April responded with laughing emojis, "Well, that's not exactly how this works. Let's wait and see when Von can go check it out, too."

"Well, I know if it's meant for us, we'll have it," Rob refuted.

Still trying to shake off the remnants of sleep, I scrolled through the conversation, surprised at how quickly things were escalating. Had I missed something? Was Rob actually as excited as I was? Or maybe it was just the jet lag making everything seem surreal. I jumped in and interrupted their flow, "I'm up. I can go see it now!"

I couldn't quite tell if it was the exhaustion speaking or if I genuinely wanted to stop the incessant buzzing of my phone. Or maybe, just maybe, I was excited at the thought of this house being the one. I noticed that if we didn't see it today, the next time Rob would be available was nearly a week away—there was no way I wanted to wait that long.

An hour later, we all pulled up to the house around the same time. The neighborhood appeared quiet and well-kept, with no noise pollution in sight. The home was nestled at the top right of a cul-de-sac. At first glance, it looked cozy, though slightly smaller than the others. Two well-manicured topiary bushes and lush shrubs bordered the entrance, and while the shutters needed a fresh coat of paint, it wasn't a deal breaker, though.

We entered through the front door instead of the two-car garage and were greeted by a carpeted stairwell leading upstairs, partnered with one decent-sized room on both sides—that's kind of small for a living or dining room, I thought. But as we continued our tour past the stairwell, we were met with a pleasant surprise: more house than the front had let on.

The beautiful kitchen featured granite countertops and stainless-steel appliances, a major improvement over the previous house. The sunroom, saturated with natural light from several floor-to-ceiling windows, led to an outdoor deck and a backyard shaded by towering trees. The wide-open family room, grounded by hardwood floors and a fireplace, radiated warmth. I could already see it as the perfect place to unwind after long days. Then there was another room—large and airy with great big windows—that immediately screamed, *my office!*

We continued upstairs to explore more bedrooms, including a master suite with a sitting area and an ensuite bathroom, before heading down to the basement. The home theater and spacious recreation area sparked a lively discussion about the endless possibilities for this space.

But as much as I admired it, something was missing. *The moment.*

As we prepared to head back upstairs, Rob paused. "Are you sure this is a walkout basement?" he asked, a hint of worry creeping into his voice as he remembered the buckets of water he'd had to bail out of his current townhouse during every heavy rain.

April, already ahead of us, turned and led the way to the back door. "I'm pretty sure, let me show you," she said, her voice calm but purposeful.

We held our breath as she unlocked the door and stepped out. The sky had dimmed, shadows lengthening across the yard. "Yup, it is!" she called back, confirming that the ground sloped away from the house. Relief washed over us both.

"Oh, wait," she added suddenly as if remembering something. "I forgot to show you this." She pointed our attention to a screened-in porch nestled under the upstairs deck, extending about seven feet out from the back of the house and about twelve feet wide. We stepped inside, and as I made my way to the center of the porch, where it happened. I saw it.

There, through the large, dusty screens framing the porch, I caught sight of the backyard. A rush of emotions hit me like a tidal wave. I gasped, clasping my hand over my mouth.

"Did you have it? The thing?" Rob asked eagerly. "Did you have *the moment*?" This wasn't just any feeling. This was *the moment*—the inexplicable but undeniable knowing that this was *our home*. It felt as if I'd been enveloped in a warm embrace of familiarity, a whisper of reassurance that this was where we were meant to be.

It felt as if I had been carrying around a transparent sheet of paper with a vision sketched on it, and when I saw this place in reality, I held that sheet up, and everything matched perfectly, down to the smallest detail. It was like my vision had finally come into sharp focus, aligning seamlessly with the reality before me. What struck me most was that this vision, just like the others, wasn't revealed after seeking it—it had been shown to me years before, not in order, but always when I needed it most."

Little did I know, Rob had already confided in April, "If Von doesn't have 'the thing,' then it's a no-go."

"April, where do we sign?" I exclaimed, tears of excitement threatening to spill over.

But finding the perfect family home on the second try was the easy part. Blending our families and navigating the unexpected challenges that followed... well, that was a completely different story.

So much hung in the balance as we pursued getting this home. We encountered countless obstacles with the financing process and faced several denials. We couldn't get approved together because of Rob's recent short sale of their home after the separation and divorce. Although I had been out of the real estate industry for years, I still had a few connections from my time on the title side. But even with those, it was nobody but God who made it possible for us to get approved and begin this new chapter together.

This experience laid a strong foundation for how our life as a couple would grow. Rob brought financial liquidity and a solid job history while I came in with my restored credit and an impressively low debt-to-income ratio (yes, I had recovered from foreclosure and bad credit!). The lender decided to take a chance on us, but I know it was God's hand working in our favor, aligning everything perfectly.

Through this journey, we learned that even with our flaws and past mistakes, we both had something valuable to contribute to building our future together. But just when we thought the approval meant smooth sailing, more delays followed. It wasn't our intention to move so quickly, but the way everything aligned, we trusted in our hearts that God would continue to work it all out—right on time, in His way. And that's what he did! "Congratulations, here are the keys!"

Having it all mapped out in my mind, I thought, "She'll get this room, he'll get that room, they'll share this room, and those two can share that one." Rob, however, didn't seem to see it the way I did.

"Why should it be that way?" he asked.

I blinked, confused. What do you mean? Didn't you hear my perfectly laid-out rationale? I thought. This was just one of many disagreements we had where our perspectives clashed. I, the "getter-doner," as Rob liked to call me, was in full organizer mode, doing what I did best—planning every detail to ensure things ran smoothly.

And though Rob appreciated my efforts, I realized quickly that my execution came off as bossy, untrusting, and independent to a fault. I wasn't used to consulting anyone. I had carried so much responsibility for so long that it felt like second nature.

Shouldn't I feel relieved? I thought. After all, here was someone who wanted to share the load and could meet me halfway. But instead of relief, I felt resistance. If I'm not making the decisions, where does that leave me? Decision-making had become my identity. And now, sharing that responsibility felt like losing a part of myself—unfamiliar, uncomfortable, and unsettling.

Does he not see my value? Who am I if I don't carry the load? These thoughts gnawed at me, and they kept resurfacing during small but pivotal moments—like the time with his daughter and the ice cream.

She had asked me for a scoop of her favorite vanilla ice cream, and I said yes without hesitation since she'd already finished dinner. But as she happily sat at the kitchen island enjoying her treat, Rob came downstairs.

"What are you doing?" he asked, clearly surprised.

"Ms. V said I could have some," she responded innocently.

I echoed her response, not understanding his reaction.

"That's funny," he said, "because I told her earlier she couldn't have any."

I looked at his daughter, and as her spoon dropped to the bowl, her posture collapsed—shoulders hunched, head bowed low, eyes drooping like a guilty puppy.

"She knows she wasn't supposed to ask you," Rob said firmly.

It was a classic case of kid manipulation, but somehow, I still felt played.

"Go to your room," he told her.

I watched her trudge off, my mind racing. Wow, I can't believe she did that. Kids really are something else. I thought we were about to share a laugh over the antics of children. Instead, Rob turned to me and said, "Von, we need to work on our communication."

What?! I was floored. "What do you mean?" I asked, frustrated. "How was I supposed to know you told her no?"

Here we go again, I thought. Does he think I'm a mind reader? I immediately retreated into my thoughts. Why didn't he give me a heads-up? Is this how things are going to be? Am I getting a lecture over ice cream? Ashton, are you here somewhere? Am I being Punk'd?

But Rob's calm patience caught me off guard. He wasn't attacking me or trying to make me feel small—he was trying to teach me that **we** had to move **in sync** as a **team**.

I started to realize the deeper struggle beneath these moments. He literally said, "We and our." Not "you and your." It wasn't about ice cream or room assignments—it was about learning to let go. It was about trusting someone else to take the lead or simply partner with you sometimes and understanding that surrendering control didn't mean losing myself.

The same patience Rob extended to me—steadfast and unwavering—was the very thing I'd prayed for. But now that it was here, I almost didn't recognize it because it didn't look the way I'd imagined. God answered my prayer, but I was too caught up in the packaging to realize it.

We often pray for things and then don't recognize the answers when they arrive because we expect them to fit into our neatly drawn expectations. But life isn't a set of perfectly cut puzzle pieces waiting to snap into place. It's more like a messy mosaic—filled with odd shapes and mismatched colors that only reveal their beauty when you step back and see the full picture.

Yes, there were challenges. The kids tested boundaries as they adjusted to new routines. Exes and extended family added unnecessary tension. Conversations about finances sparked discomfort. And there were nights when the gap between us in bed felt as wide as the ocean, with not even the brush of a pinky toe bridging the space between us.

This was the chrysalis stage of our relationship—a time of an internal struggle and a complete melting down of the familiar. It felt uncertain, dark, and messy.

There were moments when we felt stuck as if we were trapped in our old patterns, unsure how to move forward.

But just like the chrysalis, this stage was necessary. ***Growth doesn't happen without discomfort. Transformation doesn't come without tension. And new life doesn't emerge without a bit of struggle.***

The truth is, Rob wasn't trying to take my identity away—he was helping me realize that I no longer had to carry everything on my own. A new healthier identity for this stage was in the works.

We had taken a leap of faith—buying a house together, blending our families, and facing every challenge head-on. People had warned us that it was too soon. They'd told us to wait, to slow down, to reconsider. "Shouldn't you get married first to solidify commitment?" they'd ask, voices filled with concern. But we knew we were building something worth fighting for.

The chrysalis isn't a place where you go to escape—it's where you go to be remade. And sometimes, that process is uncomfortable. But discomfort is the price we pay for growth.

Transformation was happening—not in leaps and bounds, but slowly, steadily, and quietly. And soon, we would emerge—stronger, more connected, and ready for the next stage of our journey together.

But too often, we focus on what isn't developing—what isn't perfect, what hasn't yet taken shape—and in doing so, we miss what is. **We miss the slow miracle unfolding before our very eyes, the quiet and oftentimes messy, unusual, and unfamiliar beauty of becoming.**

Much like our relationship, my entrepreneurial journey was undergoing its own quiet transformation. While blending families and building a home required faith and resilience, starting a business demanded the same willingness to embrace discomfort, question norms, and trust in the unseen progress. Just as our relationship was remaking me, so too was my decision to step into the world of entrepreneurship—one careful, often messy step at a time.

Building in the Dark

Entrepreneurship

The decision to start my business was followed almost immediately by the world shutting down—the "Plandemic," as some called it. This bold leap of faith I had taken now faced an unexpected challenge. It felt like the pandemic was going to cork the bottle of my dreams before I could even take a sip. All around me, people were losing loved ones, incomes, and their sense of purpose. Lives were unraveling as if the fragile string holding everything together had suddenly snapped.

What is this? How long will it last? Is this our new normal? In the midst of it all, I wondered, how will anyone need me now? With the world in chaos, I felt trapped—just when I thought I'd finally broken free to build something meaningful. It was as if the pandemic had me stuck in this tight, stifling cocoon. How could I possibly make this work? But the truth is, I had already started setting up shop long before the world pressed pause.

My husband was leasing an office suite with multiple rooms for his business, and one of the rooms wasn't being used. That room was about to become the headquarters for Life Coach Von, LLC—the name my daughters assured me was the perfect fit. I took my time transforming it into a serene, inviting space for future clients. The décor was carefully chosen to create an atmosphere of peace where my clients could feel safe to open up and explore their potential.

Anchoring the room was a 24 x 60-inch rectangle-shaped painting framed in gold, featuring abstract waves in shades of oceanic blues and calming greens. It symbolized limitless possibilities—a reminder to my clients that, like the ocean, life has depths we have yet to explore. The silver accents throughout the room, from the sparkly rug to the carefully placed décor, were meant to ground them, providing a sense of stability in uncertain times. Affirmations and positive messages were scattered throughout, waiting to catch someone's eye and inspire them without saying a word. Even my wedding flowers, now bright and beautiful in a silver vase, brought life and personal meaning to the space.

I could envision my clients walking in, perhaps feeling lost, but leaving with a sense of clarity and direction. But just as I finished putting the final touches on this sanctuary, the world shut down. All my plans felt like they were crumbling. The season of growth I had been preparing for felt like it was slipping through my fingers.

On top of my own disappointment, my children had questions I couldn't answer. *"Why is everything shutting down? Why do we have to wear masks and gloves? Is it safe to even go outside?"* Their confusion mirrored mine. How could I comfort them when I didn't have any solid answers for myself?

I tried to find relief in small things, but the weight of it all was still pressing on me. I knew I had to dig deeper—or rather, look higher. When I shifted my focus from the chaos around me to the peace above me, everything began to change. I realized that instead of looking around for solutions, I needed to look up. God had walked with me through so many uncertain times before, and this would be no different.

That single shift—choosing faith over fear—opened my eyes to the good that could come out of this situation. Can you think of some? One thing was clear: I had been given more time to be present with my family, and that was a gift. The world, in its stillness, would also be forced to reexamine itself. Jobs, relationships, personal goals—everything was now being put on pause for re-evaluation. Many people would need guidance, and this was where I could help.

The pandemic, which initially felt like a barrier, now started to feel more like an opportunity. I realized that people would need someone to guide them through this new reality. Whether it was helping them create new income streams, navigate uncertainty, or simply find peace in the chaos, my skills and experience made me well-suited for this moment. This wasn't the path I had expected, but it was a path that could lead to incredible growth—for my clients and for me.

So, with this newfound perspective, I was ready to dive headfirst into entrepreneurship—or so I thought. But the burning question remained: Where and how do I even find my first client?

Naïve to the social media world as it related to entrepreneurship, I found myself diving into waters teeming with so-called "gurus," each eager to convince me of what I needed to start my business. You need a fancy website. You need a pristine logo and branding. You need to write a book, develop a course, create a funnel, become a speaker, build an email list... and it's going to cost you $175,000! But hey, if you do it yourself, it'll only cost $75,000—you can't beat that deal! I'll show you how! I had none of it, especially not $75k. Yet, in my desperation, I still invested in branding, websites, logos, courses, and training. Thousands and thousands of dollars later, I still didn't have a single client. Not one.

The feeling of defeat crept in again. Each week without a single inquiry made my spirit feel heavier than the last. My head, once held high with hope and faith, began to bow under the weight of my self-doubt. My eyes, which once looked upward in trust, now wandered downward—comparing myself to others in the coaching industry around me.

It was hard to admit, but if I'm being completely honest, jealousy and envy crept in, too—emotions I wasn't familiar with. I've always genuinely celebrated others' success. I'm the one people call first to share their promotions, raises, new relationships—even a lottery win—because they know I'll celebrate with them wholeheartedly. But now? Why them and not me? Why isn't it happening for me? This ugly emotion had made its home in me.

When we're in dark spaces, it's easy to fall into the trap of comparison—especially when others are excelling in areas, we desire for ourselves. But comparison is a thief of joy, and it doesn't help us move forward any faster. In fact, it does the opposite—it blinds us to our own journey and progress, adjusting our priorities to someone else's. It shifts our focus from productive self-reflection to unhealthy self-criticism. Comparison is dangerous. It drains us. What's worse is that comparison is almost always an unfair argument; it overlooks the unique factors that set us apart from those we envy.

Here's the thing about comparison: it's inherently flawed. It's about "similarities," not *exact matches*. You and the person you're comparing yourself to? You're not even playing the same game. I learned this the hard way.

I remember the time my husband bought us watches that connected to our phones. He got tired of not being able to reach me when I didn't have my phone nearby, so the watch was a practical solution. But it also became a tool to track our workouts, and we'd compare our progress. Every morning, we'd check in with each other. "I *hit 125% of my goal today!*" he'd say confidently. Meanwhile, I'd be stuck at, "*I'm still 20% short.*" I'd have to push myself more throughout the day, making sure I closed that ring.

One day, I joined him and his gym buddies for an intense workout. I was sure I'd finally hit my goal. He hit his as usual. I checked mine. *Still short.* I was blown. Finally, I asked, "*What's your goal set at?*" It turns out that his score was a full 200 points lower than mine! There I was, comparing my progress to his, completely unaware that we were playing two entirely different games. Though he wasn't intentionally drawing comparisons, and his focus wasn't on me, his bar was set lower, yet from the outside, it looked like we were striving for the same goal.

That's the danger of comparison. It's often an illusion. The outcomes might look similar, but the journeys are entirely different. The bar you've set for yourself might be higher, and that's okay. Comparison is often an illusion, a trick that makes us feel inadequate when, in fact, we're on our own unique journey.

Not only that, though this doesn't apply to this example, comparison sometimes leads to compromise. Some people achieve things by crossing lines you might not be willing to. I've heard stories, and I've been told directly by individuals what they had to do to get where they are—things I'd never want to do for the sake of success.

But, thankfully, that spirit of comparison didn't last long. Yet, at that time, it was hard to admit what I was feeling. I didn't know who to turn to. Yes, my husband was so supportive throughout this process, but I still felt alone, embarrassed, and stagnant. And just like that, I had given him an opening. The Adversary saw my darkness, my seclusion, and wasted no time trying to drag me deeper into it. His whispers reminded me of past faults and failures.

"See? You should've stayed in I.T. At least there, you wouldn't have to worry about money or finding clients. But wait, weren't you laid off? So, you weren't even good enough for I.T. either."

The enemy knows how to kick you when you're down, especially when you've left a door open. He made sure to remind me that I wasn't good enough for that last position—so why would I believe people would pay me to coach them?

I hadn't yet mentioned what had pushed me to start my own business. Though I was planning to resign after stacking my savings from trading Forex, my plans were abruptly accelerated. My company had acquired another firm, and suddenly, my position was no longer relevant.

I remember the call. *"Hey, Von, as you know, the acquisition has made some changes, and, unfortunately, your position has been terminated effective immediately. Feel free to apply for another position…"*

The word "terminated" rang in my ears. *Apply for another position?* That felt like a slap in the face! How dare they lay me off—I was planning to leave them! Have you ever felt that way? Whether it was a job or relationship, when you've planned to walk away, and they beat you to it, it stings.

Truthfully, my pride was hurt. And the Adversary was eager to exploit it. He began to whisper about all the things I'd lost—my income, the travel opportunities, the job perks. He even reminded me of the trip to Istanbul, Turkey, where I once explored new worlds and cultures and had the pleasure of bringing my husband along for the unforgettable once-in-a-lifetime experience. But now, the way things were looking, I wouldn't even be able to afford a burger off the dollar menu!

I started to fall into his trap. He threw everything in my face. All those job offers I'd turned down after being laid off. The $200k+ salaries I'd said no to. Maybe I was foolish after all, I thought. There I was—alone, with no direction, having walked away from the career I'd worked so hard to build.

But then, clarity hit me. That layoff had been an answered prayer. I'd prayed for an escape, and God had delivered it. I wasn't fulfilled in that job anymore, and deep down, I knew it. I'd started to merely exist, going through the motions of a life that no longer excited me. I didn't look forward to trips, to conferences, or even to learning new things. God had revealed the true desires of my heart, and I knew life coaching was where I felt most alive.

Aha! I was onto the Adversary's trick. He had been using the illusion of stability in my old job to make me compare it to the uncertainties of entrepreneurship. He wanted me to long for the good times, forgetting the discontent that had settled in.

Here's the reality: when you're in the dark, the enemy tries to trap you by making you forget the bigger picture. He zeroes in on small details, hoping you'll ignore everything you've accomplished just to get to this point. His tricks aren't new, but when you're caught in his web of lies and deceit, it's like getting tangled in an annoying cobweb. You try to pull it off your face, but it sticks—clinging in ways that make you think you've gotten rid of it, only for it to reappear. The more you struggle, the more it feels like it's everywhere—keeping you distracted, frustrated, and blind to the bigger plan. If you're not careful, you stop trying altogether, settling into the discomfort, forgetting there's a way out.

Yet, I had to take responsibility for opening that door. I felt stagnant and alone, and those feelings were feeding into the lies the enemy was whispering. But then, I remembered why I chose life coaching—why, in a sense, life coaching had chosen me. It made so much sense, something that flowed with little to no effort. That sense of purpose reignited my determination.

Even in this seemingly dark and still stage, a transformation was underway. Just because I couldn't see the changes yet didn't mean they weren't happening. *Sometimes, God has to temporarily blind us to our surroundings so we can focus on our internal development.* I started looking up. God began to remind me of everything I still had—my severance, my supportive husband, my calling, Him! He was giving me the desires of my heart, but it wouldn't look like what I had imagined. And I'd begun to accept that it was okay. His vision for me was beyond what I could see for myself.

As I began to refocus, it became clear that the detours and obstacles I faced were not signs of failure but lessons in disguise. I made mistakes, I invested in the wrong things, and I listened to the wrong people, but that's the work that needed to be done. Every misstep was teaching me something invaluable, and with each setback, I was inching closer to the bigger picture that God had in store for me.

Comparison, I learned, could either crush me or push me to new heights. In some ways, comparing myself to my husband's workout goals pushed me to work harder. It motivated me. So, comparison itself isn't bad; what we do with it matters.

And here, in this dark, messy cocoon phase, I realized that beneath the struggle, something beautiful was forming. This stagnant period wasn't a sign of failure—it was the beginning of something new. I was developing the mindset I needed to succeed as an entrepreneur.

Reflecting back, the health challenges I faced years earlier carried lessons that began to resonate during my entrepreneurial journey. Though the circumstances were different, the perseverance and resilience I cultivated while navigating those health trials became invaluable as I confronted the slow and often uncertain process of building a business. The connections weren't obvious at first, but over time, the parallels between these two stages of my life became impossible to ignore.

Becoming Whole

Health

Y ears had gone by since I began taking the little white "that should do it" birth control pill. But, as many of you might guess, it didn't "do it" at all—at least, not what my doctor had intended. What it did do was make me irritable, moody, hypersensitive, and, at times, utterly unhinged. I became so emotionally and mentally overwhelmed that it nearly masked my physical pain—the very pain I'd hoped to resolve, nearly eclipsed by the weight of my own thoughts and emotions. *Was that the plan all along? A diversion?* I wondered. Little did I know these "symptoms" were side effects, a hidden cost of what was supposed to be relief. Far from a miracle, this pill felt like a curse.

I was in my early twenties then, a young single mother facing life's challenges head-on. I was still finding myself, still learning the relentless demands of self-sacrifice that come with parenting—all without financial support, as my daughter's father was incarcerated. I was trying to find stable work, stay grounded, and handle a list of responsibilities that stretched far beyond my years. The last thing I needed was to feel betrayed by my own body. But I did, and that's exactly how it felt. So, there I was, putting my faith in the wisdom of a well-meaning doctor and a prescription I hoped would relieve my anguish.

Disappointment soon drove me into a maze of questions, searching for answers: scouring the internet, consulting specialists, talking to herbalists, and seeking out women who might understand my pain. Embarrassment crept in because, by this age, shouldn't I have some insight into my own body? Yet, every answer to "Why am I bleeding so heavily?" started to blur. It could be hereditary. *"Do women in your family have heavy cycles?"* they'd ask. Then came the possibilities: PCOS, thyroid issues, endometriosis, fibroids, polyps, von Willebrand disease, pelvic inflammatory disease, and even cancer. But no one had a clear answer.

The endless poking, prodding, and waiting for test results was grueling—each time hoping for relief from this unanswered mystery or bracing for the news of an incurable sentence. My patience, my pockets, and my spirit were wearing thin. Many of these tests and visits weren't covered by insurance, draining my resources even more. And since no one could pinpoint the problem, we were left to trial-and-error solutions, a twisted game of eeny, meeny, miny, moe—hoping the next try might be the answer.

They knew my condition, apart from the excruciating pain, was causing anemia. I started on iron pills, which left me so constipated that even drinking water constantly couldn't ease it. Then, of course, another medication was prescribed to manage that side effect. Taking matters into my own hands, I began researching and adding iron-rich foods to my diet. I religiously ate leafy greens and red meat, yet nothing seemed to work. Eventually, it was suspected that my body couldn't absorb iron properly, so I tried adding citrus fruits, strawberries, and tomatoes to help with absorption. Still, I found myself exhausted and defeated, avoiding any activities during my cycle for fear of an accident. I even kept a change of clothes in my car, just in case. My days were filled with discreet checks and brushes across my clothes, hoping "Mary" wouldn't come out to play. Despite following every recommendation, it wasn't enough. Physical pain and exhaustion became my normal.

When I ended up in the hospital, nearly dead, it shocked everyone—and it terrified me. I'd been training to enlist in the Navy, planning to turn my life around. It was 2011, and I saw this as my way out. After my house went into foreclosure, my credit was ruined, and I was crashing on my sister's, Leshia's, couch and floor; this seemed like the way forward. I wanted a fresh start and a better life for my daughters. My plan was to give temporary custody to my mom and sisters while I trained, and once I could, I'd bring my girls with me.

At 31, I was joining later than most. I knew I'd need to build up my physical and mental stamina to give myself the best chance. My sister Leshia joined the Army later in life, and to this day, we wonder if it contributed to her deathly health condition. I faced skepticism from my family, but I was determined. I was looking forward to showing my daughters the world, letting them experience new cultures, and breaking away from the chaos and struggles that marked our lives after their father and I separated.

Submitting my application felt like the start of something better for me and my girls. I ran at least five days a week, pushing myself through eight-mile runs. Running was my release, my way of clearing my mind and fighting the stress. I thought if I could endure this exhaustion, I'd have a better chance at surviving Navy training, especially boot camp. I knew a physical exam was required, but with all the work I'd put in, I was sure things would improve.

A few days before I was due to meet my recruiter to start the process, near the end of my run, I felt unusually winded. I was so winded I had to walk the rest of the way home, stopping frequently. *"You overdid it,"* I told myself. During these runs, I often thought about the situation I was in, what I'd put my daughters through, and I'd push myself with all my might, sometimes forgetting to breathe properly. I returned to my sister's place, took a shower, and collapsed on the couch.

All I remember from then on was lying there for days, only getting up to use the bathroom. I could hear my daughters asking, *"Mommy, what's wrong?"* and my sister saying, *"This isn't like you; you don't even look like yourself."* I was too exhausted to even chew food. By day four, when my sister asked how I was feeling, I told her it felt like an elephant was sitting on my chest—it hurt to breathe, and my heart felt like it was trying to escape. Alarmed, she insisted on taking me to the emergency room.

I don't remember the drive there. The next thing I recall is being wheeled in, struggling to answer the triage nurse's questions. I was so weak that forming a thought, let alone speaking, felt impossible. I still remember the look in the nurse's eyes as she took my vitals, her quiet yet composed alarm. They immediately escorted me to a room, hooked me up to oxygen, and took blood samples. Slowly, I felt a slight relief, as if the "elephant" on my chest had lifted its foot, granting me a small breath of ease.

Though I couldn't speak, I could pray. I was terrified, thinking of my daughters and who would care for them if I didn't make it. I knew my family would step up, but that wasn't the point. No one knew them like I did.

No one knew Tamir, my eldest, with her quiet beauty and self-awareness, navigating the challenge of discovering herself while feeling the obligation of mothering her sisters. No one understood Ta'Qara, my 7-year-old, whose self-sacrificial heart was as big as the sun and bright as the moon, balancing a timid exterior with an inner strength she seldom showed. And Ta'Rheeyn, my youngest, though only five, carried a spirit so immense that her vibrant personality and sharp humor could light up any space. *"Lord, please don't take me away from my girls."*

Dark thoughts flooded my mind. Is this punishment for not trying to make my marriage work? But I reminded myself that I'd felt released from that chapter. The war within me raged on as I lay there, the darkness threatening to consume me. Is this a sign that the Navy isn't what You have planned for me? I couldn't believe that I'd been preparing to take this step just days ago, convinced it was the path I was meant to follow.

After about an hour, a doctor entered, introduced himself, and asked, "By any chance, did you know you're anemic?" By then, I was a bit more coherent but still very weak. "Yes, I've struggled with it since I started my cycle," I replied. He shook his head and said, "No, you're severely anemic. For women, we look for hemoglobin levels to be around 12 to 15. Yours is a 4. Do you have any religious restrictions against receiving a blood transfusion?"

"No," I replied. "Good. Your condition is very critical, and a transfusion is the only way we can stabilize your levels right now."

"So, I'll be okay?" I asked, holding on to a shred of hope.

"Yes, I believe so." He went on to explain potential complications, but by then, all I wanted was to feel better. During my four-day stay, I received four units of blood. Before being discharged, I had to pass a series of treadmill stress tests to ensure my recovery was on track. I was then encouraged to follow up with a team of specialists—a gynecologist to bring my heavy menstrual under control, a cardiologist to assess any lasting effects on my heart from the prolonged anemia, and an oncologist to explore iron infusions as an option. My primary care physician would serve as the conductor, orchestrating this symphony of professionals, each playing their part in the medley of my future. Together, they formed an ensemble, a carefully tuned arrangement of care that I would have to harmonize in my life, making sure it never reached this crescendo again.

The day after I was released, I finally had time to truly rest. Hospitals don't allow for much peace with the constant poking and prodding. After squeezing my daughters a little tighter, I returned the recruiter's call—the one I was too weak and worried to answer while in the hospital. When he called to confirm our appointment, I explained what had happened, reassuring him that I was healthy enough now and would keep everything under control. But as I tried to reassure him, he gently stopped me.

"This condition makes you ineligible to enlist."

Just like that, my glimpse of hope darkened. The Navy was my answer. What am I going to do now?

The Navy had represented more than just a career shift—it had been my hope for a better future, sense of direction, and the promise of stability. Yet, in that moment of rejection, I realized that waiting and uncertainty were inevitable parts of my journey. It was a time of forced stillness, where I could no longer rely on external solutions to fill the void within me.

This forced pause, though painful, became a cocoon of its own—a space where I had no choice but to reflect, reevaluate, and begin rebuilding. Transformation often feels like this: uninvited and uncomfortable but deeply necessary.

The Quiet Power of Stillness

Patient Perspective

J ust as the caterpillar undergoes a profound transformation within the chrysalis, we also encounter significant moments in our lives—whether in relationships, entrepreneurship, or personal growth—that require us to embrace stillness and uncertainty. These are the times when the most remarkable changes occur, even if they aren't immediately visible. Let's explore how this patient perspective unfolds from a *patient perspective, which characteristics are: peace, cocooned, enigmatic, forming, creative chaos, shielded, elevated, and protected.*

Before we talk more about the chrysalis, let's take a few steps back, and let me share the fascinating science and the level of detail that is mapped out even before the formation of the chrysalis.

Before the final molt, the caterpillar undergoes behavioral changes. It stops eating and becomes restless, wandering in search of a suitable pupation site. The caterpillar looks for a location that offers protection from predators and harsh environmental conditions. This is often the underside of a sturdy branch, leaf, or other sheltered spot. The site must be stable to support the chrysalis throughout the pupation period. Branches, stems, and other firm structures are preferred. The caterpillar considers factors such as humidity, temperature, and exposure to sunlight, seeking an environment that will support successful metamorphosis.

Once a suitable site is found, the caterpillar spins a silk pad, known as a "silk button," on the selected surface. This silk is produced by glands located in the caterpillar's mouth. The caterpillar attaches itself to the silk pad using small hooks on its hind legs called "cremasters." The cremasters grip the silk pad securely. The caterpillar hangs upside down in a J-shape, signaling it is ready to begin the transformation. This position helps facilitate the final molt and the formation of the chrysalis.

Once the chrysalis forms, the caterpillar appears dormant, but nothing could be further from the truth. Inside, a process called *histolysis* begins. The caterpillar's tissues break down into a rich, nutrient-dense liquid, and the cells—known as *imaginal cells*—reorganize and bind together to form the butterfly. These once-individual cells hold the blueprint for the new identity, creating wings, antennae, and all the structures needed for the butterfly's future.

This transformation is both messy and miraculous. It's a process of deconstruction, where the old self is broken down to make way for something entirely new. But the chrysalis remains a protective shell, shielding this delicate work from outside interference. In this state, the developing butterfly is hidden, shielded from predators and distractions, allowing the transformation to occur uninterrupted.

Similarly, in our own lives, the chrysalis stage represents a time of profound internal change. On the outside, it may look like nothing is happening. People may not see the work being done, but on the inside, we are dismantling old habits, beliefs, and ways of being to create space for something greater.

There's so much to unpack here! The chrysalis stage teaches us to honor the process of becoming. It reminds us that sometimes, we must allow everything we once knew to dissolve so we can be reformed. From the outside, it may feel like life is standing still, but inside, God is orchestrating something extraordinary. The most significant changes often take place in stillness, in the quiet spaces where we are shielded and safe.

Consider the power of that stillness when you think about your cocoon moments. How many times have you felt like you were falling apart, only to realize later that you were being reshaped? These moments aren't easy—they may feel uncomfortable, even upside down—but they are essential. Growth never comes from comfort; it comes from leaning into the creative chaos, trusting that the mess is making way for something beautiful.

In my relationship with Rob, this stage unfolded as we quickly progressed to buying a house together, even though we weren't yet married. Adjusting to living together wasn't always easy—we were learning each other's habits and quirks in a shared space that often felt unfamiliar. But in that discomfort, we were being remade. The chrysalis isn't about perfection; it's about creating the foundation for something stronger and more connected.

In entrepreneurship, the chrysalis stage began when I decided to start my own business. Then the "plandemic" hit, shaking my confidence and leaving me questioning whether I had made the right decision. It felt stagnant at times, but I realized this period wasn't about visible progress but about developing the mindset I needed to succeed.

Similarly, in health, my journey through the chrysalis stage was marked by disappointment and uncertainty. After being hospitalized for severe anemia, I was denied entry into the Navy—a path I had seen as my way forward. That rejection forced me to pause, reflect, and begin reimagining my next step. In each of these areas, the chrysalis stage taught me that growth doesn't come from comfort but from trusting the messy, often painful process of becoming. Though it may feel like life is standing still, the quiet spaces of struggle are where transformation takes root.

Like the caterpillar finding the perfect place to anchor itself, we, too, must find stability to begin our transformation. *Stability doesn't mean perfection—it means being in a position where you feel safe enough to shed what no longer serves you and begin the delicate work of building what will.* And yes, sometimes that position feels upside down. But remember, your new identity requires uncomfortable positioning to help shape you for the season to come.

This stage teaches us patience, perseverance, and trust in the unseen. It's not a time to rush or resist but to allow. The chrysalis stage is about giving ourselves permission to be shielded, protected, and unhurried as the Creator forms us into what we are meant to be. It reminds us to commit everything to God and trust His timing. When life feels still and uncertain, lean into His promise: *'Commit everything you do to the Lord. Trust him, and he will help you. Be still in the presence of the Lord, and wait patiently for him to act'* (Psalm 37:5-7 NLT).

Can you think of a time in your life when you were in a chrysalis stage? A time when everything seemed to slow down, fall apart, or even stop? How did you lean into that space? What truths did you uncover about yourself, your purpose, or your faith in that stillness?

By embracing the positive perspective of the chrysalis stage, we learn to see these moments not as delays but as divine preparation for the remarkable transformations ahead.

In relationships, the chrysalis stage can represent those moments when we feel stuck or uncertain about the future. In entrepreneurship, it's the phase where ideas are incubated, refined, and transformed before they can be launched into the world. And in our health journeys, it's the critical time of recovery and rebuilding, laying the foundation for a healthier, stronger self.

Understanding and appreciating the chrysalis stage helps us recognize the value in stillness and transformation. It's a reminder that growth isn't always visible, but it's happening nonetheless, preparing us for our own emergence as something greater. Embrace these stages and trust the process, knowing that each phase is essential for the next. This stage... is a period of reflection and internal change.

Perceived Stillness

Transformation Truths

T he chrysalis stage teaches us that what appears to be still or stagnant often holds the most profound transformation. Within the cocoon of stillness, growth is happening, changes are forming, and strength is being cultivated. Are you ready to embrace the truth hidden in stillness?

Peaceful Solitude and Growth: During the pupa/chrysalis stage, we enter a state of peaceful solitude. The chrysalis provides a cocooned environment where the caterpillar can undergo its most profound transformation. Reflect on the times in your life when you needed to withdraw from the chaos to focus on personal growth. How did you navigate this space, with apprehension or appreciation? These moments of peace are essential for nurturing our inner development.

It's important to acknowledge the preparation during the caterpillar stage—the consuming and shedding—that jump-started this magnificent process. Just as the caterpillar's behavior changes as it seeks a safe place for its transformation, we, too, are given indicators that a major shift is needed in our lives. How's your appetite?

And I don't mean just for food. Are there activities or relationships you no longer crave? Are you restless, wandering, and searching for a space where you can feel both protected and stable?

Enigmatic Transformation: The chrysalis stage is enigmatic, filled with mysterious changes that are not visible from the outside. Much like this hidden process, our personal transformations often occur away from the public eye. Embrace the unknown, trusting that significant progress is being made even when it's not immediately apparent.

Forming New Beginnings: Inside the chrysalis, the caterpillar is forming its new identity as a butterfly. This stage is about creative chaos—breaking down old structures to build something entirely new. Consider how you can apply this in your life by dismantling outdated beliefs and behaviors to make way for fresh, innovative ideas and actions. Forming your new identity is a messy process. Allow God to take all you've gone through to help morph you into something new!

Shielded Development: The chrysalis shields the developing butterfly, providing protection and support during its vulnerable stage. Similarly, we require environments that offer security while we grow and change. Identify the people, places, and practices that shield you and allow for safe development. Don't feel a need to explain or express to everyone what's happening, as this may inadvertently drain your energy and change your focus. Allow the stunning transformation to be revealed at the right time. You will spend less time painting the picture because they will be able to see it.

Elevated Purpose: The pupa stage elevates the caterpillar's purpose, preparing it for a life of beauty and flight. In our own lives, periods of introspection and growth elevate our sense of purpose and direction. This stage is crucial for defining and refining your goals and aspirations.

Protected Inner Work: The transformation within the chrysalis involves intense inner work. Organs, tissues, and systems are reorganized to support the butterfly's new life. Reflect on your inner work—emotional healing, skill-building, or self-discovery. This protected phase is when you build the foundation for your future self.

Patience in Creative Chaos: The pupa stage teaches us patience amid creative chaos. The process may seem dormant and unproductive, but significant changes are happening beneath the surface. Trust the process, knowing that every moment of stillness contributes to your eventual emergence.

Reflection and Anticipation: Reflect on your life and identify your chrysalis stages. What areas are you currently cocooning for transformation? How can you embrace this period of peace and protection with patience and purpose? Understand that these stages are essential for your metamorphosis into something remarkable.

Affirmation: *"I trust the stillness, for it is within the quiet that my greatest transformation unfolds."*

By understanding and respecting the chrysalis stage, we acknowledge the importance of peaceful, protected development. This stage is the foundation upon which our future transformation is built. As we move forward, we'll explore the subsequent stages of the butterfly's life cycle and how they parallel our own experiences in relationships, entrepreneurship, and health.

A Butterfly's Transformation

"Von has been instrumental in helping me to learn to wait patiently for God's timing in my life. Through her guidance, I learned the profound beauty of waiting with grace and embracing the journey, even when the destination seemed uncertain.

When we first started working together, I was on the verge of giving up on pursuing the vision that I had for my life. I felt I was at a low point in my health, finances, and professional and personal life. I was plagued by doubts and impatience, but Von gently reminded me to find solace in the process itself, knowing that each step forward, no matter how small, was a testament to resilience and faith. Whether I was grappling with a challenging project or navigating the complexities of professional relationships, Von's words echoed in my mind, urging me to trust in the unfolding of events.

I am filled with gratitude for her presence in my life. Her unwavering belief in the power of patience and trust transformed my outlook, instilling every life trial with a sense of purpose and possibility. I've learned to cultivate patience as a virtue rather than view it as a burden. And this knowledge is something that will continue to be implemented in the days to come."

JONVOANA R. EVANS

~ Monique D. Jones

Metamorphosis Moment

*The **chrysalis stage** is a masterpiece of unseen transformation. It proves that even in stillness and shadows, something magnificent is taking shape, shattering the illusion that progress must always be visible.*

~ Life Coach Von

Chapter 7 The Emergence Stage

"Consider it pure joy, my brothers and sisters, whenever you face trials of many kinds, because you know that the testing of your faith produces perseverance. Let perseverance finish its work so that you may be mature and complete, not lacking anything. If any of you lacks wisdom, you should ask God, who gives generously to all without finding fault, and it will be given to you. But when you ask, you must believe and not doubt, because the one who doubts is like a wave of the sea, blown and tossed by the wind. That person should not expect to receive anything from the Lord. Such a person is double-minded and unstable in all they do."

James 1:2-8 (NIV)

Why Does This Hurt So Much?

Impatient Perspective

Characteristics: *struggling, disruptive, awkward, unnecessary, hard, confusing, and painful.*

People are simply unaware or take it for granted that another crucial stage unfolds between the chrysalis and the adult butterfly. *"So, we've discussed the egg, caterpillar, and chrysalis stages—what's next?"* I prompted one person. With a look of relief and certainty, they exclaimed, *"Finally! The butterfly!"* To ensure a broader perspective, I asked another, *"List the stages of the butterfly life cycle."* They confidently replied, *"Egg, caterpillar, cocoon, and butterfly."*

Curious about their depth of knowledge, I asked another participant, *"How many stages are there in the butterfly life cycle?"* They shrugged and smirked with a playful, 'shame on you' nod, answering, *"Four!"* Another even joked, *"Can I phone a friend?"* I was sure that someone would get it. Maybe I stopped asking too soon.

Each time I explained that the correct answer was actually five stages, including emergence, the response was almost always disbelief and confusion. It was as if they were rummaging through distant memories, searching for anything that could validate this outrageous claim. Only one had a light bulb moment, envisioning a picture or a diagram that confirmed what I was saying. *"Ok, I think you are right,"* they said with a half-cocked nod.

The consensus was that emergence didn't quite count as its own stage. Honestly, I couldn't blame them. I didn't fully understand its significance before I learned about all that takes place during this critical phase. But once I grasped the profound transformation that occurs in emergence—I realized it's not just a stage but the one that sets the tone for everything to follow.

"Now that you know this is a stage of the butterfly life cycle, how would you identify it?" I asked. Still puzzled by what takes place at this stage, most leaned on focusing on the definition of emergence. *"When I think of emergence, I think of coming out of something hard."* Another replied, with a balled-up face while rotating and alternating their shoulders clockwise, *"It's like trying to come out of something that has been holding you back. Like struggling to break free!"*

One went on to connect it with a real-life experience as a swimmer. *"When I was on a swim team and had to dive into deep waters, I remember having to hold my breath and use my legs and arms to help the natural buoyancy get me back to the surface more quickly. Sometimes, I even felt awkward, as if my body had to push through its soreness and all of the water just to get back to its normal environment. I can only imagine the butterfly is experiencing something similar at this stage."*

Though this phase seems unworthy of having its own stage—according to those I interviewed, let's see if you can relate to why it's worthy in all facets of life.

Breaking Free Together

Relationship

Our previous relationships often felt like curses, their shadows threatening to derail us at every turn. The bitterness of exes, the baggage we carried—at times, it seemed insurmountable. Yet, with time and perspective, those experiences began to take on new meaning. They weren't just burdens; they were blessings in disguise, offering lessons that shaped us into who we needed to be for one another. At this stage, our relationship hadn't yet taken on a fully formed identity, but it felt like we were standing on the brink of something extraordinary.

The messy, complicated moments early on weren't there to break us; they were testing what we were made of. So often, people want to run from relationships at the first sign of trouble, but what are they truly running from? Rob and I faced this question more than once. The challenges we encountered weren't red flags to retreat—they were signals of what needed attention and repair. Navigating the awkward dynamics of being bonus parents, discussing finances openly, and setting boundaries with exes were all part of the journey. These moments were opportunities to grow, both as individuals and as partners.

But it wasn't just our personal willpower or determination that carried us through—it was our faith. Deep in our souls, we knew God had brought us together for a purpose greater than ourselves. That belief strengthened us, especially when the journey felt uncertain or overwhelming. It wasn't just about proving that we could make it through; it was about honoring the charge God had bestowed upon us. This relationship wasn't just for us—it was for our children, for the legacy we wanted to leave them.

We wanted our kids to witness something different. We wanted them to see us navigate hard times with passion and conviction but also with patience, understanding, and correction. We weren't striving for perfection; we were striving to show them that love can endure, even in the face of difficulty. Every disagreement, every misstep, every breakthrough—it was all part of modeling what healthy, faith-centered love looks like. For us, the work wasn't just about coming out of this space stronger as a couple; it was about teaching our children that resilience, grace, and humility are the foundations of true strength.

Relationships often act as mirrors, reflecting areas we need to work on to grow into our best selves. For me, one of those reflections was my communication style. I thought I was a great communicator because I seemed better at it than my previous partners. But being with Rob, a natural-born therapist, revealed the cracks in that assumption. He challenged me—not to change who I was but to grow. I was the queen of shutting down, believing silence was a way to keep the peace. But as I learned, silence can fuel the fire just as much as gasoline. It wasn't until I embraced his wisdom and let go of my resistance that I began to see the transformative power of authentic communication.

Rob, too, had his mirrors to face. Though a trained professional, he sometimes struggled with adamant assumptions about what I was experiencing. He also had to learn that not everything needed to be a therapy session. I needed space to process, but I didn't know how to articulate that in a way that didn't feel dismissive or off-putting. Sometimes, I would come back days later wanting to revisit a conversation, only to find that he had assumed the matter was resolved. This became a recurring point of conflict until we implemented one of the intentional systems for communication we developed when we first met.

We called it "Where We at Wednesday" (WWaW). Every Wednesday, we would email each other, pouring out our thoughts and reflections. We shared celebrations, what we felt the other did well, areas for improvement, upcoming events, and our overall feelings about the direction of our relationship. While it might sound impersonal, it worked for us. It allowed uninterrupted expression and uninterrupted reflection. It even became a sort of relationship memoir, a record of our growth and the challenges we overcame.

Revisiting WWaW reminded us that the tools we develop along the way don't always work for every season, but they can be picked up again when needed. This realization was key to our emergence. It wasn't just about fixing what was broken; it was about refining our process, breaking through barriers, and moving closer to the relationship we envisioned—not just for ourselves but for the family we were building.

But emergence is never easy. Each breakthrough revealed new layers of resistance. The same arguments and conflicts seemed to reappear, but in truth, they were presenting new dimensions we hadn't yet addressed. Breaking through these barriers was like a butterfly struggling against the chrysalis—painful, exhausting, and at times, disheartening. But we pushed forward, knowing that these struggles were strengthening us for the next stage.

For me, one of the most significant struggles was moving from shutting down to over-communicating. Once I learned to speak up, it felt like Pandora's box had been opened. I was dumping every thought and feeling on Rob, believing it was what he wanted. But even this became a challenge. After listening to others' struggles all day as a therapist, Rob often needed time to decompress. I had to learn not just what to share but also when to share it—balancing this new dynamic required patience, grace, and understanding.

Despite these challenges, we kept moving forward. The potential of what we were building fueled us, even in the most discouraging moments. We realized that the things that were trying to hold us back—the misunderstandings, the frustrations—were preparing us for our next breakthrough.

Faith was our anchor, a steady force that grounded us through life's challenges. When the weight of life felt unbearable, Rob and I leaned into our belief that God had brought us together for a purpose greater than ourselves. We prayed—not just for our relationship to endure but to reflect a love rooted in faith, grace, and resilience. Our goal was to model for our children what navigating love with intention could look like, even in the face of adversity.

I often thought about the Proverbs 31 woman and how I aspired to embody her strength, wisdom, compassion, and faith—not as a perfect standard but as a guide to becoming the woman God called me to be. Not only, did this reflection shape how I approached my relationship with Rob, but also how I wanted to nurture

my children. I wanted to show them that love builds, heals, and uplifts, even when te
sted.

Over time, our commitment to healthy communication and faith began to influence our children. They often told us we were "relationship goals," a phrase that made us smile but also reminded us of the responsibility we carried. They saw how we loved and respected one another, even in moments of disagreement, and often sought our advice for their relationships. It was humbling to realize how much they absorbed from simply watching us.

Our desire wasn't just to strengthen our bond for ourselves—it was to leave a legacy of love for them. We wanted them to see that relationships can be messy and still be beautiful, that disagreements don't have to turn into bitterness, and that with patience and understanding, love can thrive through trials. This charge from God wasn't just about healing our relationship but creating a foundation of hope and faith for the next generation.

Then came the moment that felt like a culmination of everything we'd endured and built. When Rob got down on one knee, it wasn't just a proposal—it was a declaration of the love, resilience, and commitment that had carried us through the challenges of the past and brought us to this extraordinary point.

I remember it so vividly. He told me to dress nicely and be ready for an evening out. When he blindfolded me before we left, I didn't think much of it—Rob had done this before, planning surprises that turned into some of my favorite memories. The thought crossed my mind that this might be the moment, but I quickly shot it down, not wanting to get my hopes up. After all, I had stopped needing to anticipate it. I already felt like I had everything—the love of my life, the family we built together, and a future that already felt abundant.

When we finally stopped, he made me promise not to look, and that he would be back. After about 5 minutes, he returned and instructed me to take his hand. Stepping out of the car, I felt the brisk wind against my legs as he guided me step by step into an unfamiliar space. His voice was calm but deliberate, instructing me where to step. *"Here's a step up, another, and another. Wait—a small step now,"* he said. I had no idea where we were, but I trusted him fully.

When he finally removed the blindfold, I saw we were standing at the very place where we first met—three years to the day—the place where Niya chopped him in the throat... twice. Our closest friends, who had been there from the beginning of our journey, were there, smiling with their phones, ready to capture the moment. Still, I didn't want to assume. Rob and I had always celebrated our "Meetaversary," so this could have been just another thoughtful gesture.

But then, Rob stepped into the center of the room and began reciting a poem he had written. Line by line, he reflected on our memories, our private jokes, and the journey we had walked together. One by one, our friends handed me heart-shaped necklaces in purple and white—one for each of our daughters. It was intimate, intentional, and so very Rob. As he reached the final lines of his poem, he walked toward me, knelt, and asked, *"Would you make me the luckiest man alive..."* He opened the ring box, revealing the most beautiful, unique, sparkling ring I had ever seen.

At that moment, the weight of any prior struggles melted away. I saw our future through a lens of clarity and purpose. This wasn't just a 'yes' to Rob—it was a 'yes' to the process that refined us and the journey we had yet to embark on.

Looking back, I see how our faith in God and in each other allowed us to navigate our challenges with intention. We weren't just fighting for us—we were fighting for our family, the legacy we wanted to leave behind, and the purpose God had set before us. Each disagreement, each hard conversation, and each moment of vulnerability was like a flap of the butterfly's wings, building the strength we would need to soar together.

In the glow of that moment—saying 'yes' not just to Rob but to the life we were building—I later realized how each challenge in our relationship had secretly strengthened me for what lay ahead. The perseverance, patience, and vision we cultivated together wouldn't just shape our marriage; they were also quietly laying the groundwork for my future endeavors. Though it would come later, the world of entrepreneurship would demand these very qualities. In hindsight, I can see how weathering the storms in my personal life prepared me to face the uncertainties and opportunities that awaited me as I stepped into my entrepreneurial journey.

The Struggle That Builds

Entrepreneurship

Maybe the pandemic wasn't an unfortunate event after all. Maybe it was a funnel, narrowing my scattered thoughts and helping me focus on where I needed to be. A direct path was unfolding, one I hadn't seen before. This wasn't about setbacks; it was about catalysts—moments that would shift perspectives and lead my ideal clients to me. Their loss of income, their fear of the unknown—perhaps these weren't curses but wake-up calls. Life coaching was no longer a luxury for those who had everything together; it was becoming a necessity for those who felt their lives falling apart.

This pandemic wasn't a curse; it was a panoramic view into lives once considered too perfect or too busy to notice the frayed edges. Suddenly, the world slowed down, and the tension pulling at both ends of the rope loosened. With the pressure relieved, those once-hidden threads began to unravel, exposing truths buried beneath the surface for far too long. But this unraveling wasn't destruction; it was an opportunity. Loose threads could now be addressed, woven back together, and strengthened into something more aligned, more intentional.

Maybe their lives weren't falling apart after all. Perhaps this was their chance to reweave, to realign with what truly mattered. And in that process, they would need someone to guide them through the mess—someone like me. Not the cybersecurity systems engineer I once was, but the life coach I was becoming. Someone who navigated the murky waters of uncertainty and helped countless women find clarity during their own personal pandemics.

What's that? A glimpse of light? This subtle but long-awaited shift in my mindset felt like the warmth of the sun breaking through a long, cold night—energizing, awakening something within me that had been dormant for far too long. It gave me the strength to push forward. It reminded me that, though the circumstances were unfamiliar, the feeling of uncertainty wasn't. I had been here before—not in this exact moment, but in seasons where hope felt distant and goals seemed unattainable. And yet, every time, by staying the course, I not only reached my goals but often surpassed them.

That glimpse, that taste of light, sparked something in me. I began reflecting on other moments of resilience, like the time I tackled the grueling CISSP exam in 2015—a test that spanned 6 hours and 250 questions, requiring months of preparation. I had approached that challenge with a determination to break through, knowing it would lead to greater possibilities. And now, here I was again, staring down a new challenge, ready to rise with the same tenacity.

The approach I took during that time—reaching out to "experts" for advice—inspired some of my methods later on. We all have default moves when seeking guidance; mine was to connect with those who had already achieved what I was striving for. I turned to a social media platform for professionals, sending the same carefully crafted introductory message over and over, hoping that someone would notice my persistence and share the insight that could "change my life." After dozens of attempts and just as many rejections, one response finally came through.

His advice? "Start with low-hanging fruit." Now, people toss this phrase around casually, often not realizing how condescending it can sound. But for me, those words sparked something. At the time, earning the CISSP certification felt nearly impossible. CISSP holders typically occupied mid- to senior-level positions in information security—roles I was nowhere near qualified for...YET. With only 76,000 CISSP holders globally and a pass rate of just 50%, the odds were stacked against me. The exam was no joke—ten domains, a grueling 6-hour test, and a linear question format that left no room for error. And yet, his "recommendation," even laced with doubt, was exactly what I needed to hear.

I sacrificed time with my daughters, missed family celebrations, and devoted 9 months to studying an additional 6 hours every day while working full-time. It was exhausting, but I pressed on, fueled by determination—and maybe a bit of spite. When I finally passed the exam and earned my CISSP certification, I sent Mr. "Low-Hanging Fruit" an update. The message? I had done it. I was now a Certified Information Systems Security Professional. And yes, I'll admit, a little pettiness fueled that email—lol.

Before that, I ventured into network marketing for the first time with an MLM (Multi-level Marketing) company. This experience wasn't just about selling—it was about fully immersing myself in the product. I had to learn everything about it, adopt the lifestyle, and embody what I promoted. See, I don't promote or sell anything I haven't tried and believe in wholeheartedly. The product was new, unique, and unlike anything else on the market. If you've ever had to convince people to buy into something unfamiliar, you know you've got your work cut out for you.

I received far more no's than yeses, but even so, I kept pushing. I stayed committed, refining my approach and building trust with clients. Eventually, not only did I develop my own loyal customer base, I also built a team of over 1,500 individuals, with more than 250 based in Australia. I climbed the ranks to double-diamond—just three levels from the top. It wasn't easy, but this journey taught me that persistence, even in the face of rejection, can yield extraordinary re sults.

More and more moments came flooding in, fueling the energy I needed to break free of the darkness that had consumed me. The moment I immersed myself in this newfound energy, things began to shift. I started posting more on social media, sharing my story, and going live for hours at a time. It was the pandemic, after all, and people were willing to sit and listen—they craved connection. And there I was, finding my footing—or should I say, forming my wings?

So here I was, in the middle of this shift, wondering, *Am I going to stay consistent in proclaiming God's goodness, even when my present circumstances don't match up to the vision He's given me?* It was a test—how would I act when I had nothing? Because how I acted with nothing would likely mirror how I'd act when I had much. He was refining me for the next level.

As I became more consistent, I was invited to speak on other platforms, sharing the message that had become my calling: how to be FLY—First Loving Yourself. The pandemic had shown people they didn't know how to truly love themselves.

This message was catching on like wildfire because they desperately needed it but didn't realize it until the world slowed down.

When I launched my life coaching business, I initially figured I'd use my IT background to focus on IT career mentoring along with life coaching. Helping individuals, especially those who looked like me, break into and thrive in IT felt like a natural transition. While I did help many get their first six-figure salaries, promotions, and opportunities, it still didn't fulfill me the way I had hoped.

But the FLY concept—sharing my story of going through a divorce, foreclosure, bad credit, and initial ignorance of the importance of self-love—offered a different kind of hope. People needed someone who had been through the fire and came out on the other side. They wanted the cheat code to overcome hardship, and I was the one to help them crack it. That's when I got my first paid client.

I had been doing pro bono work initially to gain experience and figure things out. The results my clients were getting were astounding, and it became clear that I needed to start charging, not just to pay the bills, but because my work had value. I promised myself that with my first paid client, I would take a portion of that money and officially register my business—and that's exactly what I did.

I began showing up more unapologetically, sharing my journey's raw and unfiltered truth and how God had brought me through it all. I was no longer focused on just getting clients; I was doing the work that mattered. The more I reached for the light, the more the vision God had given me began to come into focus. As I tore down my own self-doubt, I started confronting the hard things—my insecurities, my limiting beliefs, my fears of how it would all come together. Once I submitted my plans to God, clarity followed.

Soon, I had consultations lined up—four or five a day. New clients and referrals were coming in left and right. I was becoming... I had become something new. I realized that, at one point, I had been so focused on making money and sustaining the lifestyle I was accustomed to that I'd lost sight of my true purpose. That's when I adopted a new mantra: *My impact produces income*. And to this day, I still believe that.

Everything that once stood in my way, everything that once confined me, ultimately made me stronger. Breaking free wasn't just a goal—it was my destiny.

These seemingly unfortunate brick walls I kept running into, chipping away at each time, were actually strengthening parts of my mind that hadn't fully matured yet. It wasn't until later that I realized each obstacle pushed me to develop the mindset I needed to truly thrive. Transitioning from a corporate job to entrepreneurship is no small feat—it tests every corner of your being and forces you to evolve in ways you never thought possible.

One of the biggest challenges is moving from security to uncertainty. In a corporate environment, you have the comfort of a steady paycheck, benefits, and a predictable routine. But as an entrepreneur, uncertainty is your new reality. Income fluctuates, and success is no longer measured by someone else's yardstick—it's a direct result of your efforts, decisions, and resilience. You're forced to embrace the unknown, to let go of the illusion of stability, and to trust that what you're building will stand the test of time.

Then, there's the shift from comfort to risk-taking. In corporate life, the risks are minimal. Your tasks are clearly defined, and you know what's expected of you. But as an entrepreneur, you're on the front line of every decision. Each choice feels like a leap off a cliff, and the stakes are high because you alone are responsible for the outcome. The weight of every decision rests squarely on your shoulders, but it also gives you the freedom to build something uniquely your own.

And finally, there's the shift from following to leading. In corporate, you're often given a direction to follow and processes to stick to. But in entrepreneurship, you set the vision and lead the charge. You're not just responsible for your business—you're responsible for leading yourself, something far more challenging than it seems.

Momentum is a powerful force—it's an equal-opportunity employer. Whether fueled by negative thoughts or positive ones, momentum doesn't discriminate. Negative thoughts can drag you down into the abyss, a spiral so fasts that you're swallowed before you realize it. But with positive thoughts, momentum can catapult you toward your goals so high that you find yourself amongst the stars, lost in the gravity of your success. It's all about where you choose to focus your energy.

And that was the real lesson in this phase of entrepreneurship. I had a choice—I could focus on everything that wasn't working, convincing myself that I was alone, trapped in the darkness of uncertainty. It was almost comforting in a way because it was familiar.

It's funny how sometimes, even though we feel stuck, we psych ourselves into believing that the unknown on the other side is far scarier. Staying there, assuming the fetal position, afraid to move forward, not realizing that this moment wasn't meant to be a final destination—it was a place of necessary restructuring—a place to fuel and prepare me for what was next.

Or I could shift my energy and perspective, focusing on what was working and what I had control over. I could let momentum pull me further into the abyss of fear, or I could harness that same momentum to rise. Either way, I would be propelled. But the direction I chose? That was entirely up to me.

As I chipped away at the walls that confined me, piece by piece, I began to emerge. My hand, once hesitant, now reached confidently for the greatness that God had placed before me. My arm stretched wide, hugging the endless possibilities that had been waiting. My face, no longer downcast, now lifted toward the future with a gaze full of hope and determination. My heartbeat steadily with newly realized courage, and my feet, once rooted in fear, took bold steps forward. Little by little, I found myself breaking free, and what I thought were obstacles standing in my way were, in reality, the very things that had been strengthening me for what was to come.

The resilience I discovered in my entrepreneurial emergence reminded me of another very different season in my life—one shaped by health challenges that demanded similar courage and tenacity. Though these events took place at entirely separate points in time, the core lesson remained: true emergence often unfolds in unexpected ways, requiring us to push through uncertainty and trust in the inner work that's taking place. What I learned from forging ahead in business would come to resonate with how I approached my physical well-being.

The Fight to FLY

Health

I was utterly exhausted. This journey wasn't just draining my finances; it was draining my spirit—and stealing my time. Time that should have been spent with what mattered most: my girls, my family, my friends, and those rare, simple pleasures of life. I longed for real relaxation, not the kind forced upon me by sheer fatigue, but the moments where I could savor quiet, read a book, or sit in peace without nodding off.

Sitting in the doctor's office, waiting to discuss the next steps, I thought about the last eight years—years disrupted by blood transfusions, monthly or even biweekly iron infusions, and a series of "let's see if this helps" medications, diets, and procedures. Each attempt offered a glimmer of relief, but I couldn't imagine spending the rest of my life like this. As I prepared to speak, I rehearsed my plea: *"Doc, take it out—all of it! I'm so over it. This is affecting my quality of life."*

My days felt like a relentless cycle of managing my cycle. I had built up a tolerance for the physical pain, but the emotional weight hung around like an unwanted ex. It was as though my life was caught between the symptoms that came before my period, the 7 to 10-day ordeal itself, and the lingering spotted reminders once it had ended. I was constantly catching up, barely able to keep up.

And then, there were my infusions. Sitting in the treatment center, surrounded by people dealing with far more severe conditions, stirred a deep internal conflict. I shared the room with those managing blood disorders like DVT—where a clot forms in deep veins, leading to pain, swelling, and discoloration—or Essential Thrombocythemia. This condition prevented their blood from clotting, leaving their skin bruised from even the slightest touch.

And yet, it was the cancer patients who filled most of the chairs around me. I'd sit in my recliner, watching them—fragile, exhausted, yet so often exuding a spirit of optimism and resilience. We regulars shared a quiet understanding, nodding to one another and offering silent support. And whenever we'd hear that one of us had surrendered and moved on, the room fell into a respectful, somber silence.

The nurses worked tirelessly to keep us comfortable in the ever-chilled room, layering us with blankets and always recommending that we bring hats and gloves. They'd bring small comforts—a packet of cheese or peanut butter crackers, graham crackers, juice, or soda—to soften the infusion blues, bridging a little gap in what otherwise felt like endless days.

This was humbling. How dare I complain? Yet, didn't I have the right to feel frustrated with my circumstances? I suppose I did—but to what end? Maybe everything I'd gone through was meant to bring me to this point. I realized it could be worse; in fact, maybe things weren't so bad at all. I began to approach my situation differently, and that small shift alone helped me navigate it in a new way. *Was that another glimpse of light?*

"Let's try an endometrial ablation," my gynecologist suggested. *"You don't want any more children, right?"* She explained that the procedure would make it nearly impossible for me to carry a child full term, even if I did conceive. My heart sank. I'd always wanted a son. And now, having met the man of my dreams, we'd talked about the possibility. I loved the two sons I now had as if they were my own, but that didn't lessen my desire to create a child together. We'd envisioned what he or she—though we hoped for a boy—might be like. What a pregnancy journey would feel like with someone I knew was my perfect match. This felt like the missing piece, the dream that would make us complete.

I had chosen to tie my tubes after my youngest daughter out of necessity. I couldn't bring another child into that marriage. And I remembered my own promise never to have multiple children by different fathers. I didn't want my kids to go through what I had: seeing a sister's father come bearing gifts, watching her leave for a "Daddy-daughter day," and not understanding why I didn't have the same. I think the doctor understood my hesitation from the long pause, the tears welling up, and the deep sigh. *"Why don't you discuss it with your partner and let me know,"* she suggested gently.

While I'd initially spoken boldly— *"Doc, take it all!"*—I realized now that it had been just talk. When I shared the doctor's recommendation with Rob, including the permanent consequences, he was similarly contemplative. His openness to the idea of another child was comforting; we hadn't talked about it recently, so knowing he still held that possibility close made me feel supported. But if we both felt torn, who would make the final call? Who would be brave enough to say, "This isn't a way to live," and to give up on a dream in exchange for my health?

Together, we decided to pray and look at this choice from every possible angle. We discussed it with open hearts and weighed the economic factors, long-term implications, timing, and whether starting over was truly right for us. How would it impact the children we already have? There were so many considerations. It took us a year to finally decide, and as difficult as it was, we concluded that our focus would be on the family we already had.

The decision, though dark, cold, and lonely in some ways, held a glimmer of hope—a small light shining on the chance for change in my health. It wasn't easy, but I was grateful to be making it with an incredibly supportive partner by my side. To say the least, after the short-lived success of the ablation, a little over a year later, it was time to discuss the final option: a hysterectomy. I thought I'd already mourned the idea of ever having another child, but deep down, I must have been holding on to a sliver of hope for an immaculate conception. By then, Rob and I had grown even closer, and with our bond deepening, I clung to the idea that our love might somehow carry a little superhuman safely through my battered womb.

But the thought of a hysterectomy wasn't only about losing the possibility of another child. It felt as if I were being asked to discard a part of my womanhood. *God, why do I have to carry so much internal conflict about this?* This decision should have been clear-cut—I despised how I felt physically, and we had tried every other option. We prayed and we fasted, but making this choice was somehow too heavy. I thought about everything that could go wrong, especially with anesthesia.

My body had responded strangely to it on multiple occasions. During my oldest daughter's birth, the epidural needed repositioning eight or nine times because it didn't work. With my second daughter, I felt a wave of agony as the anesthesia wore off abruptly during my C-section; it was like being set ablaze. They scrambled to put me under, and I took longer than expected to wake up. I had even experienced allergic reactions at the injection sites before, feeling intense burning as it coursed through me. So, my concerns were real, and Rob shared them. But ultimately, he supported my decision to go forward with the surgery.

A week before, I was so stressed about the procedure, but I knew there was no turning back. I channeled that nervous energy into preparing for my recovery, spending nearly $2,000 redecorating the first-floor room I'd be confined to, as I wouldn't be able to use the stairs leading to our master bedroom. *I might as well be comfortable,* I rationalized. It had been our oldest son's room before he left for school, and I transformed it into a healing space.

I bought a painting of peaceful waters, hung positive affirmations, and added little touches to help me stay focused. I picked out a soft, gray rug for the floor and an ottoman to help me dress with ease post-surgery. I finished the room in a single night, hoping that creating a comforting space would ease my worries.

But afterward, guilt crept in. Had I spent that money to avoid facing the real issue? I realized that rather than running from or "sitting in my feelings," I needed to sit with them. This would give me the space and permission to honestly acknowledge the disappointment and grieve this path fully without judgment. I also needed to trust that, no matter the path God would be with me.

The recovery after my hysterectomy was harsh—mentally, physically, and emotionally. But in the midst of it, I felt an unexplainable relief. For the first time in 25 years, I was free from the relentless interruptions, free to truly start living. No more hours lost in doctors' offices, no more infusions or transfusions. My time and energy were now mine to direct towards my family, my business, or simply being present in the moment. The funds that used to go toward endless treatments could now be put toward investments, trips, and even simple days out with the ones I love d.

Why did it take going through all of that to arrive here? I wondered. And I realized that sometimes you have to go deeper—way deeper—before you can finally emerge. My journey wasn't just about physical healing—it was about learning to FLY, First Loving Yourself, even when the world around me felt uncertain. Loving myself meant giving myself permission to let go of the guilt, the dreams I had to release, and the fears that tried to hold me back. Loving myself was the act of choosing life—my life—with all its complexities, imperfections, and potential.

Through the pain, I discovered that FLYing doesn't mean ignoring the hard parts of the journey; it means embracing them. It's about creating space for growth, even when it feels uncomfortable, and trusting that every choice made with intention and love will lead to a brighter, more purposeful path. As I embraced this mindset, I began to emerge—not just from surgery but from the cocoon of self-doubt and fear that had kept me grounded for so long.

And now, I was emerging. The cocoon of pain and uncertainty had held me long enough, yet it had prepared me in ways I couldn't have foreseen. I was stepping into a new light, where the weight of my past experiences strengthened me. Each challenge had woven resilience into my wings, and I could feel myself unfolding, stretching into a life of intention and purpose. I hadn't simply survived; I had been transformed.

This was my emergence—free, whole, and finally ready to soar. FLYing is more than an acronym; it's a way of being. It's the deliberate act of honoring your worth, your journey, and your growth. It's the willingness to spread your wings, even when they still feel tender, and to trust that the strength you've gained is enough to carry you forward.

As I emerged from the darkness of pain and uncertainty, I began to see the resilience I had built along the way. It wasn't just about surviving but also about stepping forward with clarity, intention, and grace. Each trial and challenge had shaped me into someone stronger, ready to face what came next.

This is the heart of the emergence stage: unveiling all that has been forming within us. It's not merely a moment of arrival but a deliberate step forward, empowered by the strength we've gained and the self-love we've nurtured. Let's explore what this stage teaches us about resilience, grace, and empowerment as we view it from a patient perspective.

A Graceful Breakthrough

Patient Perspective

The emergence stage symbolizes unveiling what has been forming within us all along. It's a period where resilience is tested and strengthened, where the challenges of breaking through are met with deliberate intention. This stage embodies the beauty of graceful progress—each step forward reflects the strength and wisdom gained through transformation. It is an essential milestone, a moment of stepping into empowerment with purpose and clarity.

This is the unveiling: ***resilient, graceful, essential, empowering***—a culmination of all that has been learned, nurtured, and prepared. Here, we honor the resilience that has carried us, the unveiling of who we are becoming, the grace with which we navigate change, and the empowerment we now embrace. Let's explore how these elements transform our personal journeys from this patient's perspective.

In this stage, the butterfly's wings attempt to expand within the confinement of the chrysalis, pressing forward and testing boundaries, with each push moving closer to freedom. The chrysalis walls, thick and resilient, are textured like woven silk and serve as a final barrier, firm yet breakable, that both contains and challenges the butterfly. With every stretch of its wings, blood flows steadily through the veins, pumping life and strength into the new wings. The butterfly strains against the walls, knowing that each push is essential to fully forming the strength it needs to fly.

Even though the wings are soft, they were designed for this very moment, formed to withstand the resistance of this escape. Each press, each attempt to break free, prepares the butterfly to face the open world beyond. What might appear as a single, brave effort is actually the culmination of time spent in stillness, hidden from the world. Just as someone might retreat from everyday life to renew their body, mind, and spirit—perhaps disconnecting from the digital world or going off-grid to find balance—the butterfly has embraced its time in the chrysalis, transforming in silence, unseen yet unwavering.

In this emergence, the butterfly must draw on every ounce of strength it has built in that quiet space, stretching, pressing, and finally breaking through. It's a delicate yet powerful process, one that shows how stillness can yield strength, how waiting can prepare us, and how transformation can ready us to fully unfold.

In our lives, emergence mirrors those times when we've had to exercise patience—whether in relationships, health, or building a business. This patience wasn't passive; it was an active, intentional investment. During those periods, we may have felt cocooned, shielded in a way that protected us as we grew and adapted, even when the transformation was invisible. And now, with the cocoon falling away, we are poised to move forward, grounded in the strength and wisdom gathered from that time of stillness.

In relationships, emergence might feel like finally understanding one another deeply, realizing that the patience invested has strengthened our bond. In health, it's a new beginning, stepping out of cycles of waiting with a body and mind prepared for what lies ahead. In business, it's the result of waiting for the right moment or growth, unveiling our work with purpose and clarity. This stage is where we test our wings, one careful step at a time, until we find our rhythm.

In the emergence stage, the struggle is real but not eternal. Every barrier you break strengthens your wings for the flight ahead. Remember, *"For our present troubles are small and won't last very long. Yet they produce for us a glory that vastly outweighs them and will last forever"* (2 Corinthians 4:17 NLT).

Emergence is about honoring what patience has cultivated within us and embracing the fullness of life with the strength we have gained. It's a reminder that every stage we've endured, every challenge and moment of waiting, was essential. Now, we have broken through the very thing that we thought was there to confine us and are ready to soar—*not merely because the time has passed but because we are* **finally** *prepared*.

Freeing Yourself

Transformation Truths

T he emergence stage challenges us to break free from what has confined us, even when the process feels painful. This is the stage where resilience is born, and we begin to embrace our potential with intention and clarity. Are you ready to explore the truth about breaking free and stepping into your purpose?

Intentional Unfolding: Emergence is a time of intentional and deliberate expansion. The butterfly doesn't simply break free from the chrysalis—it pushes through with purpose, using the strength it cultivated in stillness. Think back to the moments in your life when you were called to do the same: pushing through self-doubt, the weight of others' opinions, or the pain of trauma and unforeseen loss. Consider the times when uncertainty loomed, yet you found the courage to step forward, drawing on the resilience you built during seasons of waiting. These experiences of patience and endurance weren't wasted—they were the foundation for your emergence.

True transformation can't be rushed. It unfolds in its own time when you're ready to fully embrace all you've become. Like the butterfly, every press and every stretch is part of unveiling your new self—a self-shaped not just by the struggle but by quiet perseverance. The patience you practiced, the strength you developed, and the lessons you learned have prepared you for this moment. Now, you stand poised to emerge with purpose, honoring the transformation within and stepping boldly into the life you've been preparing for all along.

Strength Through Softness: Though the butterfly's wings may seem delicate, they are forged with the strength to endure the struggle of breaking free. Similarly, in our own emergence, we may feel vulnerable, fragile, or even unprepared—some may even label it imposter syndrome. Yet, beneath that surface of uncertainty lies an inner fortitude crafted through every trial and moment of perseverance. Acknowledge the quiet resilience within you—the strength that appears gentle yet powerful enough to carry you forward, even in the face of doubt. Trust that, like the butterfly, you have everything you need to take flight. *Remember that transformation often refines, rather than hardens, our character.*

Steady Release of Potential: The emergence stage isn't about explosive change; it's a steady, deliberate release of potential cultivated throughout the journey. In a world that glorifies overnight success, it's crucial to remember that sustainable, impactful growth unfolds gradually. True transformation demands patience and resilience as we face obstacles and use each encounter to learn, adjust, and strengthen. Like the butterfly carefully stretching its wings, we, too, need time to grow into new roles, relationships, and opportunities, gradually embracing the fullness of our potential.

Take a moment to reflect on how you can approach each step of your progress with intention. Allow yourself the space to adapt, refine, and evolve. Savor the moments of growth, however small, and honor them as essential pieces of your steady expansion into the next chapter of your journey.

Resilience from the Inside Out: The butterfly's wings gain strength as blood flows through them, nourishing and preparing them for flight. Similarly, resilience in our lives grows from within, fed by the experiences, insights, and passions we've accumulated. Think of those moments when you've woken up with a numb arm after sleeping on it, the circulation cut off, making movement almost impossible. It's only as the blood begins to flow freely again that you feel the familiar tingling, a sign that vitality is returning.

In much the same way, the "blood" in our lives—our dreams, motivations, and passions—revitalizes us, giving us the strength to move forward with purpose. When we disconnect from these sources of life, we can feel stagnant, as if our inner wings are paralyzed. But as we reconnect with what inspires and energizes us, our resilience is renewed, and our readiness to emerge grows stronger. Just as the butterfly cannot rush its readiness, we, too, must honor our own pacing, allowing this inner vitality to guide us through this stage and into our purpose.

Emerging with Grace: Emergence is about stepping forward with grace, knowing that you're ready to reveal your journey's work. This phase is much like re-entering life after a retreat or a season of deep self-reflection, carrying with you a refined purpose. Think of it as reintroducing yourself, grounded in your transformation, and gently releasing the fears or hesitations of the past.

Can you envision what your introduction as the "new you" would look like after a period of purposeful solitude? Picture yourself stepping forward, embodying a calm strength and quiet confidence. You're no longer weighed down by past doubts but instead carry a newfound clarity. Your goals are sharper, your boundaries clearer, and your actions more intentional. As you step back into life, you do so with a sense of grace, acknowledging that this journey of inner work has prepared you for each step, or would it look different?

Purposeful Expansion

As the butterfly's wings expand and strengthen, its purpose shifts from survival to exploration. Likewise, in our emergence, we are called to expand with purpose. Reflect on how you're now ready to take on new challenges and embrace opportunities. This is the time to embody your fullest self, knowing that every step is grounded in growth and intentionality.

Honoring the Journey

Emergence reminds us that every stage of transformation has meaning. As you take a flight forward, carry with you the lessons of stillness, the resilience of waiting, and the strength of preparation. Honor your journey by allowing yourself to live with renewed intention and joy, knowing you are finally ready to soar.

By embracing these truths, we celebrate the process of emergence as a steady, intentional transition into our most whole selves. This stage calls us to recognize our growth and approach life with a newfound freedom that is empowering, unveiling, essential, and graceful.

Reflection and Anticipation: Reflect on your life and identify your emergence stages. What challenges have shaped your resilience and prepared you to step into a new chapter of your life? What beliefs, habits, or fears did you have to let go of to emerge into the person you are today?

Affirmation: *"I am breaking free with resilience, stepping boldly into the light of my purpose."*

A Butterfly's Transformation

"I cannot thank Life Coach Von enough for the incredible breakthroughs I experienced during our sessions. For years, procrastination had been a significant obstacle in my life, stalling my progress and preventing me from achieving my goals. Life Coach Von helped me identify and address these issues, guiding me to "Get out of my own way" and move forward with writing my book. Her approach to setting realistic goals and not allowing failures to keep me stagnant was transformative.

With her support, I learned to navigate challenges that had previously seemed insurmountable. One of the most valuable lessons I learned was the beauty of having patience and trusting the process. Each session was a step forward, and I always looked forward to our time together. As one of her Butterfly Queens, I felt deeply inspired by her passion and dedication to personal growth. Her services were easily accessible and professional, creating an environment where I felt supported and empowered.

With Coach Von, I truly learned how to be F.L.Y. (First Loving Yourself), and I am grateful for the confidence and clarity she has helped me achieve. She is a markable life coach, and I highly recommend her to anyone seeking personal growth and lasting change."

~Ty C.

Metamorphosis Moment

*The **emergence stage** is where resilience is forged. It reveals that the barriers we break through are not obstacles but essential pressures designed to shape us for the heights we are meant to reach.*

~ Life Coach Von

Chapter 8 The Adult Butterfly Stage

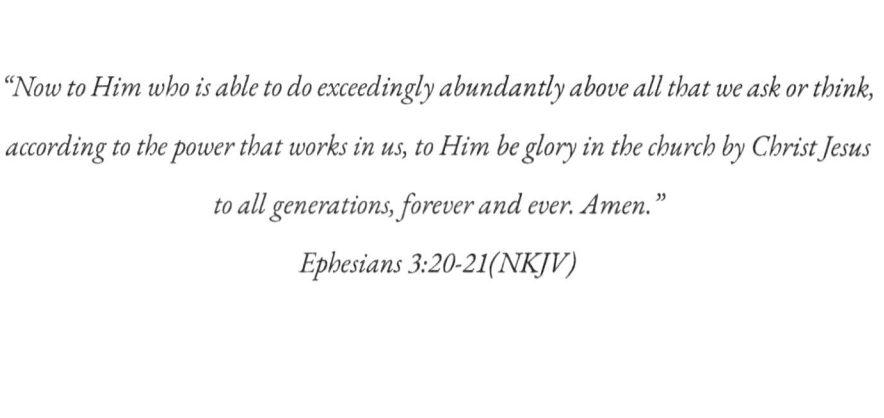

"Now to Him who is able to do exceedingly abundantly above all that we ask or think, according to the power that works in us, to Him be glory in the church by Christ Jesus to all generations, forever and ever. Amen."

Ephesians 3:20-21(NKJV)

Finally, I've Made It... Or Have I?

Impatient Perspective

Characteristics: *Restless, Eager, Unsettled, Impulsive, Expectant, Rushed, Hungry, Overwhelmed, Driven, Impatient*

When people think about the butterfly stage, there's often a sense of excitement and anticipation. This is the stage they've been waiting for—the final form, the moment of beauty and freedom. *"So, we've talked about the egg, caterpillar, chrysalis, and emergence stages. What comes after that?"* I asked one participant. With a confident grin, they replied, *"The butterfly, of course! This is it!"* Another chimed in, *"This is the best part! It's finally free to fly and live its life. The hard part is over!"*

Many people view the adult butterfly stage as the pinnacle of the journey. *"This is the moment I've been waiting for!"* one participant exclaimed. *"Butterflies are so beautiful and graceful. It's inspiring to see them flying freely, just enjoying life!"*

Another added, *"It's like they've earned their wings after all that struggle—it's time to shine!"*

While their enthusiasm was undeniable, I couldn't help but notice a common misconception: the idea that this stage marks the end of the journey, the point where all the work is done. To challenge this perspective, I asked, *"Do you think the butterfly immediately knows what to do once it's out there?"* After a pause, someone admitted, *"I guess I never thought about that. I just assumed it was instinct, but maybe it's not that simple."*

The reality of the adult butterfly stage is often overlooked. Yes, the butterfly has emerged in all its beauty, but this is not the end—it's a new beginning. Its wings, though fully formed, are still soft and need time to gain strength. The butterfly must learn to navigate its new environment, find nectar to fuel its energy, and avoid predators. The work is far from over; in fact, it's just beginning.

One person related this stage to their own experience of starting a new chapter in life: *"I remember getting my dream job and thinking I'd finally made it. But once I started, I realized I still had so much to learn. It felt like I was starting all over again."*

Another likened it to becoming a parent: *"I thought having a baby would be the happily-ever-after moment. But then the reality hit—sleepless nights, constant demands, and figuring things out as I went. It wasn't the end of the journey but the start of a whole new one."*

It's fascinating how people view this stage with excitement and pride but often miss the reality that it comes with its own challenges. There's a tendency to think of this stage as a destination, yet impatience often creeps in as we realize there's still work to be done. The truth is, the adult butterfly stage is not about resting on past accomplishments but about adapting, growing, and stepping fully into your potential.

This stage isn't just about arriving or showcasing beauty—it's about learning how to navigate your new identity and purpose. It's a time of exploration, resilience, and discovery. The wings are formed, but the journey has only just begun.

The Beauty of Commitment

Relationship

W e had agreed that we wouldn't prolong our engagement and would get married the following year. It wouldn't be anything big and fancy as we both had already been there and done that before. We wanted it to be intimate with our family and close friends. Initially, the plans were to have a destination wedding—I wanted to do Turks & Caicos—but once we realized the cost would be a year's worth of tuition to put one of our children through college, we decided that a stateside wedding would do.

Believe it or not, we decided to have our wedding at home: an intimate gathering of 80 people in our basement. Our large open floor plan became the canvas for a vision of warmth and beauty that felt like stepping into an enchanted garden, requiring our special guests to step out of their world and into ours. As you descended the basement stairs, your path was graced with intertwining green foliage and delicately dimmed string lights, creating a magical glow that danced along the railing.

At the bottom of the stairs, you turned a soft corner, where the aisle awaited—a shimmering path adorned with rhinestone tea lights nestled within a garland of lush, green, ivory-colored foliage. It was as though the earth itself had paved the way, guiding you toward the heart of the celebration.

To the left, a lake of 45 folding chairs cloaked in black linen created a striking contrast against the softness of the room. At the far end, our pool table, which doubled as table tennis, a symbol of everyday life, had been transformed into a breathtaking display. Draped in pure white satin fabric that spilled to the floor, it held a custom centerpiece I'd masterfully crafted. Bursts of orange, white, fuchsia, and turquoise flowers emerged from the arrangement, kissed with the soft light-embedded accents of sparkling rhinestone butterflies. A clear glass vase, grounded by earthy tones of brown and orange glass rocks, held everything together—a reflection of the vibrant yet grounded essence of our union.

It wasn't just a room. It was an atmosphere, a feeling, a glimpse into the love and care we had poured into this day. Every detail whispered a story of intention, reflecting both our journey and the beauty of the moment we were about to share.

To the right was a section of 20 chairs that sat our children in the front row, and a couple of rows thereafter were our parents, grandparents, sisters, and brothers. Off on an angle to the right of them sat another special group of friends we considered family, as they too were a very special part of our union: April and Khary, the couple whose event started it all; Niya, the one who chopped him in the throat, twice; Adrienne and Russell, a couple that we adored; Tynisha and Lisa, my best friends—more like sisters—my godparents, and a few others.

At the heart of the room, about three feet beyond the main wall, stood a 16-foot cove that transformed into our enchanting altar. The backdrop was our freshly painted, pristine white fireplace, now elevated to a masterpiece. Its front opening was adorned with a delicate ribbon of silver rhinestones, catching and reflecting the light with every glance. At the same time, a plush, white, rectangular rug lay softly in front, inviting reverence and warmth.

Framing this sacred space on each side were white Roman-style columns that stood proudly at about three feet tall. They were wrapped in cascading greenery intertwined with glowing string lights as if nature itself had embraced the moment. Seated on the columns were glass vases, two feet tall, filled with shimmering white-water beads that radiated light from within. Large, vibrant fuchsia flower balls were resting on top that were delicately kissed with matching rhinestone butterflies.

At the center of the fireplace mantle stood another one of these vases, its presence adorned by a trail of green foliage draping gracefully along its length. To complete this scene of pure intention, ceiling-to-floor stringed crystals framed both sides of the fireplace like a curtain of light, catching every sparkle and movement in the room. Together, these elements wove a tapestry of elegance and symbolism, grounding us in the beauty of what this altar represented—our sacred vows, our shared dreams, and the foundation of love we had built together.

At the altar, surrounded by everything we had built and everyone who had witnessed our journey, we were reminded of the butterfly's purpose. It emerges not to rest but to live, to pollinate, to bring beauty and value to the world around it. This stage of our lives felt like stepping into that purpose. We weren't just taking vows for ourselves but committing to being an example of love, growth, and resilience for others—especially our children.

In the front-right corner of the shimmering crystal strings stood a round table, 3½ feet in diameter, draped in a white fitted spandex tablecloth that seamlessly hugged its curves. Overlaid diagonally was a long piece of sparkly turquoise tulle, its shimmer resembling a calm ocean under the sun. This layer was beautifully contrasted by a vibrant layer of fuchsia tulle. Together, these layers created an ethereal blend of elegance and celebration.

This table became the sacred stage for our communion. At its center was a single, exquisitely shaped glass bottle, designed with a graceful hollow center for easy handling and refinement. It held the wine—a rich symbol of our union—radiating an understated beauty as the light danced across its surface. Accompanying it were three matching long-stemmed crystal red wine glasses: mine on the left engraved with the word "hope," his on the right "believe," and the center one "love." Co-starring the sacred stage, framed in silver, is our statement of unity that I wrote, and we would recite it before taking communion. Its title: "Two Cups Pouring into One."

The idea was that our parents would each pour wine from the bottle into our separate "cups," and then we each would pour the contents of our "cups" into the center one, labeled "love." It read:

"As God has poured into me, I pour all into us. As we sip from the same cup, we speak with the same mouth. As we sip from the same cup, we love with the same heart. As we sip from the same cup, we live for the same God whom we place first in our lives and our union. Amen."

This symbolism reflected our faith and our desire to root our marriage in God's love and guidance. We wanted our children to see this not as a ceremonial moment but as an example of a God-centered union—one where patience, understanding, and purpose were the foundation.

Behind the poem was one of my favorite paintings that Rob had created for me. It was of a tall male body figure and a shorter woman body figure in a strong but reassuring embrace. Where their heads would be were replaced with wide bowls, and there was an overflow of a water-like substance pouring out of his bowl into hers, cascading down in abundance.

To us, this painting represented God's intended design for marriage—a union of overflowing love and strength grounded in faith. Every detail of this setup spoke to the profound meaning of the moment, combining visual splendor with heartfelt intention. It set the tone for a ritual and experience that would forever remain in our hearts.

When coming up with this theme, I thought about our sessions in marital counseling with Pastor James Marshall. As we both worked through things we hadn't openly discussed with others, it revealed that there was always more work to be done. There was one question he asked that we toiled over, and once we came to a decision, it would—and has—set the tone for how we would be towards one another and the level of commitment we would put into our marriage.

"So, Doc," as he would refer to Robert, *"you are a change maker in your community, helping individuals navigate the mental health space, an upstanding father and man to those who have the pleasure of knowing you. And Von, I don't know a lot about you, but according to what I've gathered during our time together and based*

on what you and Rob both shared, you are an intelligent woman," referring to my position at the time as a cybersecurity systems engineer, *"a passionate woman of God, having a heart to help people, and an outstanding mother. You are both individual powerhouses and have so much to offer those around you."*

We both took delight in his reflection of us. Then, the question that stumped us was, *"What would you want to be known for as a couple?"* We sat in silence before looking at each other, trying to find the answer, as we had never really discussed that question. Somewhat uncomfortable with the silence, we looked at each other and started to throw out possible answers. *"Well, the Power Couple is what people have said."* *"Or, the Empowerment Couple,"* as it reflected Rob's company name, Empowerment Counseling, and Training Services, but also pointed to how we loved empowering people. We both threw up the white flag, saying, *"We don't know. We will need to think about it."*

First and foremost, meant praying about it. At this point, we had already been practicing abstinence for six months and agreed t continue until the wedding, a total of eight months. During this time, we developed a practice of not only abstaining but also strategically reading the Bible, praying, and fasting together. We learned so much about each other, our relationship, and God during this period.

During our final counseling session, we thought we had an answer for Pastor Marshall, but we realized God hadn't fully revealed it yet. At first, we didn't understand why. Then, it became clear: ***God wasn't going to hand us the answer—He entrusted us to create it.*** He made us individuals, each with unique gifts and talents, and brought us together to define our identity as a couple. The beauty was that there wasn't one "right way." As long as we kept Him at the center and ensured He got the glory, how our union manifested in the world was ours to shape. We just knew that we wanted others to see God through us.

This understanding reinforced the essence of the adult butterfly stage: embracing who we had become, not just individually, but as a union. It was no longer about waiting to be told or shown what to do. It was about stepping into the purpose we had been prepared for, trusting the foundation of our faith to guide our steps.

This public display of beauty and splendor was a physical manifestation of the culmination of our journey. From our humble beginnings to the messy and challenging stages of growth, it reflected the moments of stagnation that tested us and the resilience that carried us through. It was the result of pushing past the hard times, bruised egos, and pride along the way.

Each phase of our relationship mirrored the butterfly's journey—from the fragile potential of the egg to the consumption and shedding of the caterpillar to the stillness and surrender of the cocoon. And now, at the altar, we stood in our emergence, our wings strengthened by the trials we had endured. This was the beginning of our adult butterfly stage—a stage not defined by perfection but by purpose, where we would soar together, guided by the lessons and love that had shaped us.

All that we had experienced had come to this moment of what we had been privately working on, and we were elated to take our vows in front of our children, our family, close friends, and most importantly, God. There weren't too many things I was sure of when I pursued them in my life. But marrying Robert was one thing I had no doubt about.

People often take this moment in their relationship as the pinnacle, but Rob and I knew very well that we had honestly just arrived at the base of an uphill battle, for lack of better words. There was still so much effort to be put forth—a term he preferred over "work." But the beauty in it all? We weren't just building for ourselves; we were building a legacy—for our children to see what it meant to navigate life and love with God at the center. And the joy of it? We were doing it as Dr. and Mrs. Evans.

Here we are, seven years later, deeply grateful for the work...effort that brought us through all those stages to become who we are today. Just recently, we saw Pastor Marshall at church. It had been a couple of years since we last connected, as he had been elevated to a phenomenal position with a global organization. When he greeted Robert and me, his warmth was unmistakable. *"I am so proud of you two!"* he exclaimed. *"I follow y'all on social media, and y'all are doing your thing! I'm so happy for you both. Keep up the amazing work!"*

I can only imagine what it must feel like for him—after counseling and marrying so many couples—to witness the manifestation of a union walking in its God-given purpose. To see two people not only surviving but thriving, doing the work we were meant to do.

As individuals and as a couple, we have taken so many lessons learned about parenting, co-parenting, building businesses, intimacy, finances, navigating the dynamics of a blended family, maintaining self-identity within marriage, and prioritizing physical, mental, spiritual, and emotional health. We've strived to live in a way that makes our children proud. And through it all, our prayer continues to be that when people see us, they will also see God through us.

We've traveled, spoken on stages, appeared on radio shows, podcasts, and TV programs, and participated in webinars, conferences, retreats, and workshops. In doing so, we've pollinated singles, divorced individuals, and married couples, offering them hope, direction, understanding, and love as they navigate their own stages of life and relationships.

And though we celebrate the beauty of what's been built so far, the work is far from over. Much like the adult butterfly, this stage is not the end of the journey—it's the beginning. It's the start of a life lived with intention, purpose, and the strength earned through every trial.

Wherever you are on your journey, know this: *the Adult Butterfly stage isn't about reaching a destination; it's about stepping into your purpose, letting the world see your wings, and offering hope to those who are still in their cocoons.*

Embracing the adult butterfly stage in our relationship taught me that living with intention, purpose, and a spirit of generosity wasn't limited to our personal lives. The very qualities that helped us thrive as a couple—resilience, vision, and a commitment to contributing something meaningful—also shaped how I approached my career. Reflecting on how we'd grown together, I could see these lessons guiding me as I continued to develop my entrepreneurial endeavors, ensuring that my business, too, would become a vessel for spreading hope and elevating others.

FLYing With Purpose

Entrepreneurship

T he 14-Day FLY Challenge was a popular online initiative I hosted to expose women to the undeniable benefits and power of First Loving Yourself. Through a private group, participants received 14 pages from my 45-Day FLY Journal—an interactive resource filled with affirmations, journal prompts, and creative tasks for self-discovery and fulfillment. For 14 days, at no cost, women connected, shared their experiences, and held each other accountable.

The activities ranged from lighthearted tasks, like dressing up and taking selfies or reminiscing about a favorite childhood game, to deeply introspective challenges. One activity, "Mirror, Mirror," encouraged participants to look at themselves in the mirror and say aloud what they truly felt.

One moment during the Challenge remains etched in my memory. A participant shared how the activity broke her. She had avoided looking at herself for years, only to discover, at that moment, how much pain she was carrying. *"I cried for hours,"* she said, *"but it felt like I was finally releasing the weight of decades."* Her vulnerability reminded me of my journey and the deep healing that happens when we confront ourselves with honesty and grace. It wasn't just about the tasks but about creating space for transformation.

Another, "Shower Me with Love," required them to spend 15 minutes in the shower or tub saying only positive things about themselves. These exercises invited women to face truths they often avoided, fostering a deeper connection with themselves.

The challenge offered more than just tasks—it provided a glimpse into life coaching with me. Many participants realized how much easier it was to prioritize others over themselves, often to their detriment. They saw how the absence of boundaries created chaos—not just with others but within themselves. For the first time, many felt seen, heard, understood, and supported without judgment. They recognized the weight of societal and personal expectations—the belief that their identities were tied to their titles and roles as moms, wives, daughters, employees, or volunteers.

This challenge became more than a 14-day journey; it became a movement. Women began sharing the #FLY message far and wide, returning to participate multiple times, still uncovering new aspects of themselves. I saw clearly how my career transitions, rejections, and identity struggles had prepared me for this moment. It all made sense now—the confusion, the perseverance, and the lessons learned. I had found my tribe, and they had found me.

From this foundation, I developed affirmation cards, webinars, and workshops that expanded the FLY concept. As the challenge gained momentum, the ripple effects became undeniable. Women experienced personal growth and became better partners, mothers, and friends. They grew more confident, patient, and optimistic, and those around them noticed. Their transformations affirmed the very reason I had started this work: to help women discover themselves and the power they held within.

But as the world shifted, so did the challenge. It went from 14 days to 7, then 3, and eventually faded altogether. I questioned everything. Had the message lost its relevance? Was it time for me to pivot? As always, I turned to prayer, and clarity followed. The core message remained—First Loving Yourself—but its presentation needed to evolve.

This evolution led me to reflect on a common thread among participants. Many women expressed frustration with their jobs and felt trapped, unfulfilled, and undervalued. They spent most of their waking hours commuting, working, and worrying about work, yearning for more meaning in their lives. Meanwhile, I was living in my passion and purpose. I loved creating content, connecting with clients, and witnessing their breakthroughs and "aha" moments during our sessions. I knew I had to help these women find the same joy and alignment in their lives.

This realization led me to focus on helping women align their actions with their authenticity. Through my work as a Passion & Purpose Coach, I guided women in exploring their core values and strengths, encouraging them to build careers rooted in fulfillment rather than obligation. One client shared, *"For the first time in my life, I feel like I'm choosing a path that's mine, not one handed to me."*

And yet, as fulfilling as this work was, a new pattern emerged. More than half of the women I coached felt called to life coaching. Between their inquiries and my own reflection, I realized another pivot was needed. Thus, the FLY Life Coaching Academy was born. Watching aspiring coaches find their niche, build their platforms, and master transformational skills became a new source of fulfillment. The Academy wasn't just about certification—it was about empowering individuals to walk boldly in their purpose. Watching them transform—gaining clarity, confidence, and purpose—was deeply rewarding. What started as a personal mission to empower women evolved into empowering coaches who could, in turn, empower others.

But my vision didn't stop there. I wanted these coaches to thrive not just as individuals but as part of a larger mission. I pursued government certifications and formed partnerships with corporations and wellness organizations. This led to the creation of the FLY Life Coaching Association, which provided a professional platform for coaches to leverage their skills. By funneling clients through strategic partnerships, I helped coaches in diverse niches—relationships, health, leadership, emotional wellness, and more—make meaningful impacts. Each partnership, each coach, and each client became a testament to the power of collaboration.

Reflecting on this journey, I see how every stage—every pivot and challenge—has shaped my path today. I see how it has reshaped and revived me. The path was never linear, but the beauty was in the evolution. The beauty isn't just in the results but in the process, the lessons learned, and the transformations along the way.

As fulfilling as my journey has been, *I've learned that living with purpose is not a destination—it's a lifelong commitment.* The excitement comes in knowing there's always more ahead, even if I don't know exactly what it looks like. Each new chapter brings unexpected lessons and opportunities, and I've learned to embrace them all with an open heart.

This openness keeps the experience of FLYing with purpose vibrant and fresh. God's plans are far greater than anything I could design on my own, and surrendering to His guidance brings a peace that nothing else can. There's something incredible about living in the moment, trusting that each step forward—no matter how uncertain—has a purpose.

I often remind myself that my time here is predetermined. But even within that reality, I am determined to pollinate the world with the gifts God has entrusted to me. I know He didn't design me to merely exist; He created me to contribute, uplift, and be a part of His divine masterpiece. Every client I coach, every stage I step onto, and every connection I make become a part of that contribution.

As I learned to trust God's timing and align my actions with His will, I realized that patience doesn't mean standing still. It means being deliberate and thoughtful, even when the path ahead feels unclear. Don't mistake patience for procrastination. This is where our gifts and talents intersect with a need, thus destined to cause impact.

These moments of waiting were pivotal in positioning me to fully embrace my calling—not just as a life coach but as a facilitator of transformation for others. Waiting with intention is not about idly passing the time; it's about preparing, growing, and trusting that each step—when taken in faith—will lead you closer to the purpose God has designed for you.

This shift in perspective helped me see that the periods of "waiting" in my business were actually seasons of preparation, shaping me for what was to come.

And as much as I've been blessed to teach and guide others, I remain a student—always listening, learning, and surrendering. I pray daily for clarity on where to go next, how to serve, and how to continue aligning my actions with His will. I know that as long as I stay tethered to His guidance, my impact will ripple far beyond what I can imagine.

The adult butterfly stage isn't about arriving; it's about beginning anew. It's about using everything you've gained through your journey to live with intention and purpose. The beauty isn't in the destination—it's in the flight itself.

Wherever you are on your journey, I invite you to embrace it fully. Maybe you're chasing a goal, convinced that achieving it will bring fulfillment. Or maybe you're afraid to take the next step, uncertain of what lies ahead. The flight of the adult butterfly reminds us that every stage has value, and the journey itself holds the greatest beauty.

Accepting my calling and sharing my gifts through entrepreneurship taught me that purpose can be expressed in countless ways. It shaped how I show up for others and approach each new opportunity with faith and intention. Reflecting on this, I began to see that the same mindset could guide how I cared for my well-being. Just as I had nurtured my business into something meaningful, I would now find myself nurturing my health—transforming challenges into platforms for growth, understanding, and the chance to help others navigate their journeys.

Living in Full Color

Health

About four months after my hysterectomy, I felt better than I had ever imagined! That ridiculous craving for ice—something I had dealt with for years—had completely dissipated. I was totally convinced it was directly connected to my anemia, even though so many doctors denied it could be a symptom. For the first time in decades, I felt energized. I actually looked forward to working out!

And let's not even talk about the time that was suddenly awarded back to me. No more long, exhausting doctor visits. No more transfusions. No more days spent recovering from debilitating fatigue. I had all this time and energy—two luxuries I hadn't experienced in a long time. And the money? That, too, was a new gift—no more endless expenses for menstrual products, medications, or hospital bills.

But with all this newfound freedom, I quickly found myself overwhelmed. I had dreamed of this moment for so long—so why did it feel so unfamiliar? As quickly as I embraced this new version of myself, I felt myself slipping into something I couldn't quite name. Shouldn't I have it all figured out by now? After all, I had yearned for this moment for so long.

Looking back, I realize that we often focus so intently on accomplishing a goal that we don't consider what life will look like once we achieve it. I had placed so much unwarranted pressure on myself to know exactly what this "new me" would look like and how I'd embrace her. On one hand, I was eager to share with others just how liberating it was to finally be period-free. On the other hand, I felt debilitated by the weight of emotions I hadn't expected. What if I'd made the wrong choice? Could I have tried harder, waited longer, or explored more alternatives?

Yet deep down, I knew I was exactly where I needed to be. What I didn't realize at the time was that I was experiencing post-hysterectomy syndrome. It was like post-partum—a period of adjustment that mirrored the emotional highs and lows, physical changes, and identity shifts new mothers often face. This wasn't just a physical recovery but a reckoning of who I was becoming. I had to give myself grace—a reminder that progress doesn't happen all at once.

In those moments, I found myself leaning into grace—not the kind that allows you to sidestep the work but the kind that creates room for imperfection. I had to silence the unreasonable expectations I had placed on myself to always have the answers. *Von, you've never encountered this before; how were you supposed to know?* I would remind myself. Those internal dialogues became a tool to confront my ego and shift my focus from shame to solutions.

Once I embraced grace, I began to seek guidance—not just from God but from others He had placed in my life. Time and again, I realized how often we pray for answers, expecting a divine voice, when sometimes God sends His wisdom through the people and circumstances around us. A conversation with a friend, a chance encounter, or even an unexpected suggestion on my phone became moments of clarity. I learned to keep my heart and mind open, knowing that guidance often comes in forms we least expect.

With that guidance came growth, but not in the way I anticipated. It wasn't about having everything figured out. It was about taking small, intentional steps toward a life I hadn't fully envisioned yet. I began listing all the things I could now do—things that anemia and my cycle had stolen from me. I could finally go swimming without worry, spend more quality time with my family, and save money for vacations instead of medical expenses. For the first time in years, I could see possibilities beyond limitations.

But just as I started to settle into this new rhythm, another challenge emerged: early-onset menopause. Hot flashes, restless nights, weight gain, low libido, hormonal acne, brain fog—all of it hit me like a ton of bricks. My husband noticed, too. His unwavering support became a lifeline as I navigated this next phase. Rather than seeing it as another hurdle, I reframed it as part of the journey. "To whom much is given, much is required," I reminded myself. This was the "much" that came with the gift of renewed health.

Through trial and error, I discovered bio-identical hormone replacement therapy (BHRT)—a solution that changed everything. My body and mind began to find balance again. But more than that, I realized how important it was to share this discovery, especially within the Black community, where these conversations are too often silenced. I made it my mission to educate and empower women, offering them hope and options I never knew existed before my journey.

This stage—living in full color—has taught me that life isn't about reaching a finish line. It's about painting the picture along the way, using every challenge, obstacle, and triumph as brushstrokes on the canvas. Whether filled with joy or struggle, each moment adds depth and meaning. My masterpiece isn't complete yet, but I trust that as long as I keep surrendering to God's plan, the colors will continue to unfold in ways more beautiful than I can imagine.

Much like the adult butterfly, this stage of life isn't about resting on the beauty of transformation. It's about embracing the responsibility to pollinate—to share what I've learned and inspire growth in others. The butterfly's work is delicate yet essential, fleeting yet impactful. Similarly, my life's work is about giving back, sharing wisdom, and contributing to a greater purpose. My wings, strengthened by the trials I've endured, carry me forward with intention, grace, and resilience.

Living in full color means accepting that this is not the end of the journey—it's the beginning of a life lived with purpose. It's a call to action to use the gifts I've been given to pollinate the world around me. As I embrace this stage, I'm reminded that every vibrant hue on my canvas—every experience, every challenge—was necessary to create a masterpiece uniquely my own. This is the essence of the adult butterfly: not simply existing in beauty but living with intention, spreading hope, and leaving a legacy of love and purpose.

Each challenge and triumph had been a deliberate stroke of God's artistry, painting my life's canvas with hues I never expected. And now, as I step into this phase, I see that living in full color isn't about resting on what's been created—it's about carrying the beauty forward, sharing it with the world, and inspiring growth in others.

This is the essence of the adult butterfly stage: not simply existing but thriving with purpose. It's a stage where the lessons of patience and resilience blossom into acts of splendor and significance, leaving an indelible mark on the lives we touch. Let's explore how this stage teaches us to embrace and extend our beauty through the patient perspective.

Work Worth Doing

Patient Perspective

T his stage is where everything comes together—the culmination of every struggle, every lesson, and every moment of transformation. The adult butterfly stage is not just about celebrating the beauty of what you've become; it's about sharing it with the world. This is the moment where the patience, resilience, and growth cultivated in the earlier stages radiate outward, offering light and inspiration to others. It's the stage where your journey's colorful and beautiful essence becomes evident—not just to you but to everyone around you.

Now, the world begins to benefit from your purposeful existence, your capacity to create splendor, and the delicate yet powerful act of pollination as you leave your mark on the spaces you touch. This is not just an arrival; it's the start of something even greater—a commencement of living fully in alignment with your purpose. Let's explore how the patience of this stage reveals its ultimate reward: ***colorful, beautiful, purposeful, splendor, delicate, commencement, and pollination.***

We often yearn for Stage 5, imagining it as the destination—the moment we've "arrived," where all our struggles are behind us and the beauty of transformation is fully realized. But the truth is, this stage is not the end; it's an evolution. It invites us to step into purpose with grace, humility, and intention, carrying forward everything we've learned along the way.

As humans, we often attach glory to a destination or appearance, believing that if we don't look or feel a certain way, we haven't "made it." We rush toward what we perceive as the finish line, desperate to arrive at a place where all our struggles dissolve. Yet, the adult butterfly reminds us that transformation is ongoing and purposeful. Stage 5 is not a conclusion—it's an invitation to live with intention and to serve with the gifts cultivated in the journey.

When the butterfly emerges, it is delicate and vulnerable. Its wings, still soft and damp, must unfold and harden before they can carry it into the air. This process is not instant—it requires patience and intention. The butterfly must allow blood to circulate through its wings, nourishing and strengthening them for flight. We often face this same tension in our lives: We've broken free from our cocoons, but we're not yet ready to soar.

The butterfly doesn't rush this stage; it instinctively knows time is required to prepare for what's next. Similarly, we must give ourselves grace in these moments of adjustment. Life after transformation can feel overwhelming. Suddenly, you're faced with choices, responsibilities, and the expectation to "have it all together." However, rushing into flight without readiness can lead to failure or burnout.

Reflect on a time when you felt overwhelmed after achieving something you deeply desired. Perhaps you prayed for the opportunity, worked tirelessly for it, and celebrated its arrival—only to feel unsure of what to do next. This is the adult butterfly stage: a season of adjustment where the work is far from over but shifts into a new form. It's not about breaking through barriers anymore; it's about pollination—using what you've gained to uplift, serve, and inspire the world with the purpose cultivated through your journey.

The butterfly's life isn't just about being beautiful or admired; it's about fulfilling its role in the ecosystem. Pollination is its purpose. Every flower it touches and every seed it helps spread contribute to something greater than itself. In the same way, our transformation is meant to impact others. Our journey of growth, pain, and perseverance equips us to serve, inspire, and lead. This stage calls us to step boldly into our roles, embracing the beauty and responsibility of our transformation.

Similarly, the adult butterfly stage in my journey has been about stepping boldly into my purpose and using my transformation to impact others. In my relationship, this stage began with our decision not to prolong our engagement, moving forward with a beautiful wedding day that marked the start of our intentional life together. Through marital counseling, we identified what we wanted to be known for as a couple and have since embraced the work of showing up in the world as a unified team, living out our purpose together.

In entrepreneurship, the adult butterfly stage has been a time of evolution—watching my business thrive while adapting to new focuses and opportunities. Every shift has played a role in fulfilling my intended purpose, reminding me that the journey is as valuable as the destination.

In health, the joy of life after my hysterectomy gave way to navigating the challenges of early-onset menopause. While the confusion of this stage tested me, it also empowered me to educate and inspire others, turning my trials into tools for transformation. Like the butterfly, my wings have been strengthened by these experiences, carrying me forward with grace and resilience. This stage is not the end of the journey—it's the beginning of living with intention, spreading hope, and leaving a legacy of love and purpose. The adult butterfly teaches us that every stage of life equips us to pollinate the world around us, creating something greater than ourselves.

Yet, despite its vibrant colors and seemingly effortless flight, the butterfly remains vulnerable. Predators, weather, and environmental changes are constant challenges. Likewise, we must navigate life's unpredictability, staying grounded in the lessons of previous stages. The adult butterfly stage reminds us to be resilient and humble, knowing that we've been prepared for this moment but still need God's guidance to sustain us.

The adult butterfly stage is not just about basking in beauty or your achievements —it's a powerful reminder that transformation is about purposeful living—using your wings to reach new heights and pollinate the world with hope, love, and wisdom. Embrace this stage with patience, humility, and gratitude, trusting that you're exactly where you need to be.

Pollination with Purpose

Transformation Truths

The adult butterfly reminds us that transformation is not the end but the beginning of purposeful living. Each lesson learned and strength gained is meant to be shared, leaving a lasting impact on the world around us. Are you ready to hear the truth about living purposefully and spreading hope to others?

Purposeful Flight and Impact: The adult butterfly stage is where transformation meets purpose. This stage invites you to take flight with intention, spreading the beauty and wisdom gained through your journey. Much like the butterfly, which pollinates the world as it moves, we, too, are called to impact those around us with the lessons and growth we've cultivated. Reflect on how you can use your gifts to serve others and leave a lasting legacy.

Sustained Growth and Humility: Becoming a butterfly doesn't mean the work is over—it signifies a new type of growth. The butterfly must sustain its strength, find nourishment, and adapt to new challenges. Similarly, this stage is about maintaining your progress with humility and recognizing that transformation is ongoing. Reflect on how you can remain grounded while stepping into your purpose. Who or what keeps you aligned with your values?

Spreading Seeds of Impact: Pollination is one of the butterfly's most profound contributions, and in our lives, it symbolizes using our experiences to inspire and uplift others. Your journey wasn't just for you—it was also for the people who will be touched by your story, your work, and your impact. Think about how your transformation can become a seed for someone else's growth. How are you spreading hope, knowledge, or love through your actions? Ask yourself, what am I carrying forward from the earlier stages of my journey?

Embracing Your New Form: The butterfly's wings are vibrant and unique, shaped by the struggles it endured in earlier stages. This stage encourages you to embrace the new version of yourself with confidence. Acknowledge your progress and accept that you're equipped to navigate this phase. What aspects of your growth are you most proud of? How can you fully own and honor this new version of yourself? Are you giving yourself the grace to adjust to this new chapter, or are you rushing to meet external expectations?

Living Intentionally and Worshipfully: The butterfly doesn't just fly aimlessly; it lives with intention, pollinating and contributing to the ecosystem. In our lives, this stage reminds us to align our actions with a higher purpose. By keeping God at the center, your transformation becomes an act of worship—a way to glorify Him through the life you live. What steps can you take to ensure your actions reflect gratitude and purpose?

Reflection and Continued Alignment: Reflect on your current stage as an adult butterfly. How are you using the lessons of the previous stages to live intentionally and make an impact? What areas of your life could still use realignment with your purpose? Remember, flying as a butterfly isn't about perfection—it's about progress, pollination, and purposeful living. Who or what are you pollinating in this season? How are you maintaining strength and seeking nourishment in this new stage? What legacy do you want to leave as a testament to your transformation?

Affirmation: *"I am living with intention, spreading hope and purpose to the world around me."*

A Butterfly's Transformation

"Meeting my life coach, Life Coach Von, was a transformative experience that began with a simple yet profound question: "What if all of your desires work out?" At a time when I was entangled with limiting beliefs and negative self-talk, her words would pinch me so hard or even pierce through the fog of doubt and fear that clouded my mind. I realized I had been crafting stories in my head that were drenched in negativity, believing that I was unworthy or incapable of achieving my dreams. Her question challenged me to envision a different narrative—one where my desires were not only possible but probable.

Even someone with degrees and degrees, we tend to need some help, too. It was the spark that ignited a journey of self-discovery and growth. Throughout our sessions, she guided me with patience, and aside-eye, and a deep understanding of the importance of trusting the process. She taught me to reframe my thoughts and replace self-criticism with self-compassion.

Her support was unwavering, and her belief in my potential was a beacon of hope. As I learned to quiet the negative voices and embrace a more positive outlook, I felt a profound shift within myself. Her coaching has been a catalyst for change in my life,

helping me cultivate a mindset of possibility and resilience. I am endlessly grateful for

her guidance, which has empowered me to rewrite my story and step confidently into

a future filled with hope and promise."

   ~Dr. Katashia

Metamorphosis Moment

The adult butterfly stage is a revelation of purpose fulfilled. It reminds us that transformation is not merely for ourselves but for the world we touch, pollinating lives with the wisdom and beauty forged in our journey.

~ Life Coach Von

Chapter 9 The Rebirth

"Therefore, if any man be in Christ, he is a new creature: old things are passed away; behold, all thingsare become new."

2 Corinthians 5:17 (KJV)

A New Beginning

Emerging as a butterfly is not the end—it's a new beginning. The transformation is complete, but the journey of living with this new identity has just begun. The same is true for us after we've undergone seasons of growth and waiting.

We must step forward boldly, embracing the new and trusting God's plan for what's next. Just thinking about the progression of my relationship and previously being married, though I just knew I was meant to be "a wife" and knew I would be great at it, I had to redefine what being Rob's wife would look like.

I took all the things we had been through, the disagreements, the joys, the necessary conversations, the late-night cuddling talks, the business meetings, goals and dreams, the heated arguments, and pulled lessons from them all to embrace this "new identity," that didn't do away with the old me. It = did away with the old habits that did not support this new identity and what I was called to do.

But stepping into the "new you" isn't always easy. There's a temptation to look back, to question whether the transformation was real or sustainable. There's a vulnerability in stepping forward because it's unfamiliar and untested. It's here, in this delicate yet powerful moment, that trust becomes your lifeline.

Jeremiah 17:7-8 reminds us of God's promise, *"But blessed is the one who trusts in the Lord, whose confidence is in Him. They will be like a tree planted by the water that sends out its roots by the stream. It does not fear when heat comes; its leaves are always green. It has no worries in a year of drought and never fails to bear fruit."*

Let's break this down. Trusting in the Lord anchors us. It grounds us in the truth that He is reliable, unchanging, and faithful. Think about the seasons in your life where you leaned on everything *but* God—jobs, relationships, material possessions—and saw how they wavered. Yet God? He never falters. Even in moments when the answers seem unclear and when the path feels shaky, He's working all things for your good.

Transformation often comes with doubt. Can I handle this? Am I ready for what's next? This is where the concept of rebirth becomes both practical and spiritual. Your transformation wasn't an accident—it was intentional, divinely orchestrated for the purpose God has for you.

The butterfly teaches us an essential lesson in this phase: its new identity wasn't an overnight miracle. Inside the chrysalis, imaginal cells reorganize to form its wings, antennae, and every intricate detail. Similarly, everything you've experienced has prepared you for this moment. God was creating a masterpiece in you, even when it felt like chaos.

As you step into this new season, you must make practical and spiritual shifts. This is where you claim your new identity and live in alignment with who God says you are. Philippians 1:6 reminds us: *"He who began a good work in you will carry it on to completion until the day of Christ Jesus."*

Transformation is not a one-time event; it's a continuous journey of becoming. Think of this moment not as a finish line but as a starting point. You've been renewed, but now comes the work of walking confidently in this renewal.

You may feel delicate, like the butterfly's wings right after emerging, but remember—they were designed to withstand flight. Similarly, God has equipped you with strength for the journey ahead.

Lamentations 3:24 declares, *"The Lord is my portion; therefore, I will wait for Him."* Trust isn't passive—it's active, requiring us to move forward even when the road ahead isn't fully visible. As you embrace your rebirth, hold tightly to the hope that has carried you this far. Your hope is not misplaced. It's rooted in the One who made you and knows the plans He has for you.

Let go of the doubts that whisper, "This isn't real," or "You'll return to your old ways." Instead, declare the truth of Isaiah 26:3, *"You will keep in perfect peace those whose minds are steadfast because they trust in you."* Focus your mind on His promises, and let peace be your guide.

Rebirth also calls us to live with intention. The butterfly doesn't emerge to exist; it has a role to play in pollination, in the continuation of life. So do you. Your journey wasn't just for your benefit—it's meant to inspire, encourage, and uplift others.

According to Ephesians 1:4, *"For He chose us in Him before the creation of the world to be holy and blameless in His sight."* You were chosen for this. Live it boldly.

It is written in scripture: "*To whom much is given, much is required, and from the one who has been entrusted with much, much more will be asked.*" Reflecting on this truth helps keep me grounded. We are responsible for what we've been given—our gifts, our talents, and, yes, even our trials. I've come to understand that everything I've been entrusted with, including the difficult and dark times, has a purpose far beyond myself.

God doesn't just bless us for our own benefit; He blesses us so that we can bless others. Even the burdens He allows us to carry are often meant to equip us for greater things—to strengthen us, refine us, and prepare us to be a beacon of light for those walking through their own darkness. Each trial, each moment of waiting, is an opportunity for God to work in and through us, offering hope and purpose to others.

For me, this perspective has been transformational. It reminds me that the waiting isn't wasted. The tears I've sown, the faith I've had to muster, and the patience I've been called to practice are all part of the harvest He's preparing. And just as I've always required much of God—dreaming big, praying bold prayers, and trusting Him with my deepest desires—I understand that He also requires much of me. Faith, patience, and service to others are all part of the exchange.

So, I ask you: How much do you require of God? What big dreams, bold goals, or deeply held desires are you entrusting to Him? How many tears are you sowing, and how much faith are you willing to give? If you're anything like me, you've always required much of God, and the reaping will be a testament to what you've endured.

What He blesses you with, or what might feel like a burden now, isn't just for you. It's part of a larger purpose—one that connects you to the world in a way only you can fulfill. Trust the process, even in the waiting. Trust that He's preparing not only your blessing but also your ability to handle the "much more" that will be required when it comes. Let this truth be a source of hope and strength: your waiting is not in vain, and your harvest will be worth it.

This rebirth is not the end—it's the start of a new cycle. Each step forward is a chance to honor God, live purposefully, and embrace the beauty of becoming. As you continue this journey, remember: the process is never wasted—it's all working for your good and His glory.

Metamorphosis Moment

"When we are foolish, we want to conquer the world; when we are wise, we want to conquer ourselves."

~ John Maxwell, A Self-aware Leader

Chapter 10 The Cycle

"The Lord is not slow to fulfill his promise as some count slowness, but is patient toward you, not wishing that any should perish, but that all should reach repentance."

2 Peter 3:9 ESV

Where the Cycle Leads

Life's cycles are not just repetitions—they are movements forward, shaping us and leading us to something greater. Have you ever stopped to recognize the cycles in your life? Not all cycles are "bad." Some may feel unhelpful or unproductive, but even a cycle can propel you forward. Just as the butterfly's life is a cycle of transformation, growth, and purpose, so are our lives. Each stage is essential—fragile in its own way—yet undeniably necessary for the next step.

The situation you were born into, the challenges you've faced, and even the unexpected detours connect to what you are meant to nurture and grow in your life. But uncovering that connection requires patience—patience to embrace the process and trust that every step, no matter how small or uncertain, is leading you toward something greater. Each stage brings its own unique challenges, lessons, and blessings, much like life itself. Yet, so often, we resist the process.

Why? Because we want to rush through it. We want to skip to the "good part"—the end result, the destination. We shy away from the discomfort, uncertainty, and waiting that are part of the journey. We don't see the value in the struggle. But here's the truth: without the struggle, there is no growth. Without the process, there is no transformation.

Impatience has a sneaky way of creeping in and derailing us. It whispers lies, telling us we're behind, missing out, or failing. It urges us to act hastily, to take shortcuts, or to move before we're ready. And when we fall for it, impatience doesn't just slow us down—it brings destruction, distractions, and delays.

Think about it: how often have you made decisions out of impatience, only to regret them later? Maybe you rushed into a relationship because you were tired of being alone, only to find yourself in a draining situation. Maybe you jumped into a business opportunity before you were fully prepared, and it collapsed. Maybe you abandoned a goal too soon because the results didn't come quickly enough. Impatience tricks us into treating symptoms instead of addressing root causes. It pushes us to act without understanding and rush without preparation.

I know this because I've been there. I've been the one praying for a harvest without planting the seeds. I've been the one trying to understand God's plan before being willing to do what He was calling me to do. And let me tell you, that approach doesn't work. Understanding can wait—obedience cannot.

One of the hardest lessons I've learned is that waiting is not a punishment; it's preparation. God doesn't ask us to wait to make us suffer. He asks us to wait because He's working on us and for us. Waiting isn't about standing still—it's about surrendering. It's about saying, "God, I trust Your timing more than I trust my own." It's about planting the seed of faith and letting Him provide the increase.

But that kind of surrender isn't easy, is it? It feels counterintuitive, like letting go of control. And maybe that's the point. Maybe waiting is God's way of reminding us that we're not in control—and that's okay. Because while we're busy trying to figure it all out, He's already worked it out.

But let's be honest—waiting, trusting, and surrendering? They're easier said than done. As human beings, we have an innate desire to feel like we're doing something and that we're in control. And the truth is, there is something you can do. When the waiting feels unbearable, when uncertainty threatens to overwhelm you—go into PRAYER.

Growing up, I was taught about the power of prayer—that it changes things, moves God's heart, and aligns us with His will. "The prayer of a righteous person is powerful and effective" (James 5:16). But over time, I've come to understand that prayer is about more than asking for what we want or waiting for God to act. It's about transformation. It's about surrendering control and allowing God to work in and through us.

But here's the catch: Waiting in prayer isn't an excuse to be passive. It doesn't mean sitting on your hands, doing nothing, and expecting God to handle everything. Waiting in prayer is active—a partnership with God, a time to reflect, prepare, and align your steps with His purpose. It's a process of growth and faith-building that requires intentionality.

To help guide you through this waiting process, I developed an acronym: PRAYER—Purposefully, Reflectively, Actively, Yieldingly, Earnestly, and Reverently. These six elements are designed to transform how you wait, turning frustration into faith and stagnation into preparation.

Let me break it down for you:

Purposefully: When you wait purposefully, you're not just sitting idle—you're searching for God's direction and leaning on His strength. *'Search for the Lord and for his strength; continually seek him'* (Psalm 105:4 NLT). Waiting becomes an act of faith, not frustration.

Reflectively: Waiting is a time to look inward and reflect on God's past faithfulness in your life. Think about how He has carried you through before, and trust that He will do it again. *"When you pass through the waters, I will be with you; and when you pass through the rivers, they will not sweep over you"* (Isaiah 43:2). Reflection builds trust and reminds you of His unchanging presence.

Actively: Waiting doesn't mean being idle. It means taking steps toward growth, even when you can't see the full picture. Ask yourself, *What can I do in this season that aligns with God's purpose for me?* *"Commit to the Lord whatever you do, and he will establish your plans"* (Proverbs 16:3). Progress often begins with preparation.

Yieldingly: Surrender your timeline and trust that God's timing is perfect. Let go of the urge to control every outcome and allow Him to guide you. *"Trust in the Lord with all your heart and lean not on your own understanding; in all your ways submit to him, and he will make your paths straight"* (Proverbs 3:5-6). Yielding isn't giving up—it's letting go.

Earnestly: Approach prayer with sincerity and faith, believing that God hears you and will answer in His perfect way. *"Do not be anxious about anything, but in every situation, by prayer and petition, with thanksgiving, present your requests to God"* (Philippians 4:6). Earnest prayer shifts your focus from worry to worship.

Reverently: Honor the process of waiting as sacred, knowing that God's plan is unfolding exactly as it should. Be still and know that He is God. *"He has made* *everything beautiful in its time"* (Ecclesiastes 3:11). Reverence brings peace to the waiting, reminding you that His timing is never wasted.

These elements work together to make your waiting in prayer intentional and transformative. Waiting in this way isn't passive—it's preparation. It's an active demonstration of faith, trusting that God's promises are worth the wait. As 2 Peter 3:8 (NLT) reminds us: "But you must not forget this one thing, dear friends: A day is like a thousand years to the Lord, and a thousand years is like a day." God's timing is perfect, even when it feels slow to us. He has not forgotten about you.

As you pray and reflect, I hope this journey through the butterfly's life cycle has given you a new perspective. As each stage of the butterfly's transformation is essential, so are the stages in our lives. Each one brings its own lessons, challenges, and opportunities for growth. Let's take a moment to revisit them, not just as phases of the butterfly's life but as metaphors for our own.

The egg represents potential. It's a fragile beginning, full of possibilities that haven't yet been realized. But it's also a time of waiting and nurturing—an essential period where everything necessary for life is already present, though unseen. In our lives, the egg stage reminds us that even when nothing seems to be happening, the groundwork is being laid. It's a call to trust in the beauty of small beginnings and to protect what is precious—whether it's an idea, a dream, or a vision waiting to be birthed.

Remember, the egg doesn't rush to hatch. It waits patiently until the conditions are right. Are you rushing through your beginnings? Or are you giving them the time and care they need to grow?

The caterpillar embodies consumption and shedding. It devours everything in its path, building up the resources it needs for transformation. But its growth isn't without discomfort—it repeatedly outgrows its own skin, shedding what no longer fits.

In our lives, the caterpillar stage is all about preparation. It's messy, relentless, and sometimes uncomfortable but deeply necessary. This is the phase where we absorb what nourishes us—wisdom, skills, faith—and release what holds us back. Ask yourself: What are you consuming? Is it truly helping you grow, or is it weighing you down? What are you willing to shed to make room for what's next?

Then comes the chrysalis—a stage where magic happens quietly. On the outside, it seems as though nothing is happening, but inside, everything is breaking down and being rebuilt. It's a time of profound stillness, surrender, and transformation. The chrysalis offers protection, but it's also a place of vulnerability.

Growth often requires us to step back, be still, and trust the process. It's not about doing more; it's about becoming more. Have you embraced the cocoon moments in your life? Or are you resisting the stillness, afraid of what it might reveal? Remember, the darkness isn't your enemy—it's your incubator. The most profound transformations often happen in the quietest, most unseen places.

Emergence is the struggle to break free. It's messy, uncomfortable, and requires every ounce of strength you've built. But it's also the stage that prepares you for what's next. Without the struggle, the butterfly's wings wouldn't be strong enough to fly.

In our lives, emergence reminds us that struggle isn't the end—it's the beginning. It's where we discover our strength, test the limits of our growth, and step into the new identity we've been preparing for. What struggles are you facing right now? Instead of asking, "Why is this happening?" ask yourself, "What is this preparing me for?"

The adult butterfly stage is where we find purpose and fulfillment. The butterfly's life is beautiful but fleeting. Its purpose is to pollinate, reproduce, and contribute to the life cycle. Even in its short existence, it fulfills its destiny with grace and intention.

In our lives, the adult butterfly stage is about living out our purpose. It's a time to share what we've learned, to give back, and to create something lasting. But it's also a reminder to savor the moment and embrace the beauty of now. Are you living with intention? Are you using your wings to pollinate the world with the gifts God has given you? This stage isn't just about being—it's about giving.

Each stage in the butterfly's life cycle offers a profound lesson for our own. Together, they remind us that transformation is never easy but always worth it. Trust the process, for every stage—no matter how small, messy, or challenging—is preparing you for something greater.

The butterfly's life cycle is a remarkable journey of adaptation, survival, and purpose. Each stage presents unique challenges, yet each one is necessary. Much like a farmer does not harvest all year, there is a time to rest, plant, grow, and reap. Each season plays a vital role in preparing us for what's next.

The waiting becomes a blessing when you stop focusing on what's missing and start preparing for what's coming. Because, while I was waiting on God, He was waiting on me.

The butterfly's life cycle is a profound metaphor for our own journeys. Each stage—no matter how small, slow, or messy—has a purpose. And just like the butterfly, we are called to go through each phase, trusting that the process is shaping us for something greater.

So, wherever you are in your cycle, know this: You are not stuck. You are becoming. Embrace the egg. Consume and shed like the caterpillar. Surrender in the chrysalis. Struggle in the emergence. Fly as the butterfly.

As I reflect on my journey—through relationship challenges, entrepreneurial struggles, health crises, and moments where I doubted God's presence—I now see that it all played out beautifully for my good and His glory.

While I was waiting on God to answer my prayer, He was waiting for me to be still and listen.

While I was waiting on God to get me out of messy situations, He was waiting for me to learn my lesson.

While I was waiting on God to send me my king, He was waiting for me to heal and work on my attitude so I wouldn't spread infection.

While I was waiting on God to bless my finances, He was waiting for me to be a good steward of what I already had.

While I was waiting on God to heal my heart, He was waiting for me to forgive.

While I was waiting on God to give me peace, He was waiting for me to let go of some people, places, and things.

While I was waiting on God to make my dreams come true, He was waiting on me to believe.

And even now, while I was waiting on God—nearly a year past my desired timeline—for the words to complete this book, He was waiting on me to live through the experiences He intended for me to share.

The same is true for you. When you finally take flight, you'll see—because while you're waiting on God, He's waiting on you.

As one cycle concludes and another begins, we are continually shaped, refined, and led closer to our purpose. The beauty lies not just in the cycle itself but in where the cycle leads.

Metamorphosis Moment

"Be patient but persistent, remembering it's a process, celebrating the progress."

~ Life Coach Von

Special Note to Aspiring Life Coaches and World Changers

*I*f you've been searching for a sign, longing for clarity, or questioning your purpose, let me remind you: God has already equipped you for the work He's called you to do. So many of you are waiting for a miraculous sign from God to prove, show, or confirm that you were "called." But the proof is already within your daily life—it's all the confirmation you need.

God reveals His purpose through His Word and challenges you to look inward to see how He has uniquely made you. "For we are His workmanship, created in Christ Jesus for good works, which God prepared beforehand, that we should walk in them" (Ephesians 2:10). It's not enough to simply say, "I want to help people." Be intentional about the specific group of people He has called you to serve and the way He has designed you to serve them. "Each of you should use whatever gift you have received to serve others, as faithful stewards of God's grace in its various forms" (1 Peter 4:10). You don't need a large platform to make a significant impact.

Don't worry about those who won't listen or respond—it's all about the ones who will. They are waiting for you. Your unique experiences, strengths, and even your scars *are the very tools God uses to transform lives. Someone is praying for the answers you carry.*

There's no need to be ashamed or concerned about your past because God will use every part of it to pollinate the plenty. "And we know that in all things God works for the good of those who love Him, who have been called according to His purpose" (Romans 8:28). **I am convinced that the highest form of worship is operating in how our Heavenly Father intended.**

Remember, this journey isn't about perfection—it's about showing up faithfully, every day, in obedience and love. Everything you've experienced is for your good and God's glory. You don't have to have it all figured out. For we are reminded that His grace is all we need and His power works best in weakness (2 Corinthians 12:9). Trust that as you take each step, God will guide the way, just as He has promised. While you are waiting on God, He is working and waiting on you! Now, go be great in all of your stages!

With Heartfelt Gratitude,

~Jonvoana R. Evans aka Life Coach Von

The Cycle Resources Guide

The resources and tools in this section, whether mentioned throughout the book or exclusive to this guide, are designed to support you on your journey. Use them as a quick reference whenever worry, anxiety, or impatience begins to creep in. Better yet, incorporate one or more into your daily routine to stay proactive and resilient.

As the saying goes, "The best time to fix the roof is when the sun is shining." Addressing areas of growth and preparing during peaceful times can minimize the potential for deeper challenges or setbacks when storms arise. This guide will help you reinforce the lessons you've learned and maintain your progress.

PRAYER Acronym (Chapter 10)

Purposefully, Reflectively, Actively, Yieldingly, Earnestly, and Reverently. A guide to waiting in prayer with intention and faith.

Stages of the Butterfly Life Cycle (Back Section)

Egg, Caterpillar, Chrysalis, Emergence, Adult Butterfly: Insights for identifying where you are in life.

A Butterfly's Prayer of Surrender (Back Section)

A heartfelt prayer to help you release control, embrace trust, and align with God's will during seasons of waiting.

Patience in Practice (Back Section)

A reflective tool to help you align with your current stage and purpose, including the FLY Performance Curve to assess stress and productivity levels.

FLY Performance Curve: Finding Your Balance (Within "Patience in Practice")

A visual guide to understanding the relationship between stress effort and performance, helping you identify whether you're in the Chilling Zone, Flow Zone, Overwhelmed Zone, or Burnout Zone.

Grounded in Gratitude (Back Section)

An interactive tool to help you explore how practicing gratitude can enhance mindfulness, cultivate patience, and shift your focus to what's working well in your life.

While They Waited: Lessons in Patience from the Bible

Inspiring stories of faith, perseverance, and trust, highlighting how waiting on God's timing can lead to transformation and fulfilled promises.

Affirming The Cycle

Affirmations to help shift your perspective as you go through The Cycle.

The Butterfly Atrium Creed

A powerful declaration of self-commitment designed to inspire confidence, resilience, and alignment with your highest potential.

Stages of the Butterfly Life Cycle: Quick Reference Guide

L ife is a series of cycles, and the butterfly's journey offers a profound metaphor for our transformation. Each stage—from the egg to the adult butterfly—carries unique challenges, lessons, and opportunities for growth. This guide is a quick reference to help you identify where you are in your journey and navigate each stage with intention and faith.

1. Egg: The Beginning

Theme: Potential and Purpose

The egg represents the start of something new. Protect it fiercely—this is where potential begins to take root. It's a stage of hidden promise where the groundwork for growth is being laid. In this phase, focus on planting seeds of faith and nurturing the dreams and desires God has placed in your heart.

2. Caterpillar: Consuming and Shedding

Theme: Preparation and Growth

The caterpillar is marked by consuming what will nourish it and shedding what no longer serves. This is a time of active preparation and learning. Embrace this stage by intentionally acquiring the specific knowledge, habits, and skills needed for your journey. Remember, it's not just about consuming more—it's about consuming what aligns with your purpose and equips you for transformation.

3. Chrysalis: Stillness and Transformation

Theme: Reflection and Inner Work

The chrysalis stage is one of solitude and stillness—a season of deep, often unseen transformation where old structures are broken down to create something entirely new. This is also where distractions may try to derail your progress. Be intentional about creating time for stillness and reflection, even when it feels uncomfortable. Trust the process, knowing that profound growth often happens in the quietest and most challenging moments.

4. Emergence: Breaking Through

Theme: Resilience and Expansion

Emergence is the stage where you begin to break free from past constraints. Resistance will likely feel constant, but it's necessary for building your strength. Each struggle refines you, preparing you for the life you were created to live. Keep pushing forward with faith, knowing that every effort brings you closer to your purpose.

5. Adult Butterfly: Purpose and Pollination

Theme: Living with Intention

The butterfly stage is about using your gifts to serve and inspire others. This is where you embrace your full potential and pollinate the world with the beauty and purpose cultivated through your journey. Stay humble in this transformation, keeping God at the center. Let your growth become an extension of your worship and a testimony to His faithfulness.

Note: *For a deeper dive into each stage, including practical insights and personal reflections, refer to Chapters 4 through 8.*

A Butterfly's Prayer of Surrender

Sometimes, in the midst of painful or anxious waiting, it's hard to find the words to pray. The emotions feel too heavy, and the uncertainty is too overwhelming. In those moments, let this prayer guide your heart. Use it as is, or add your own words to make it personal as you seek God's strength and direction to navigate this season of waiting.

My Heavenly Father,

Hallowed be Your name. Today, I come before You with open hands and a humbled heart, ready to surrender all that weighs me down. I acknowledge that Your plans for me are greater than anything I could imagine, and I trust that Your timing is perfect.

Lord, I release my need to control the outcomes. I let go of the fear, the doubt, and the impatience that often cloud my faith. Instead, I choose to rest in Your promises, knowing that You are always working for my good.

Help me find peace in the waiting, Father. Teach me to embrace this season as an opportunity to grow, learn, and draw closer to You. Help me to be sensitive to Your voice, which will block out all others that are not of You. May I not waste this time worrying about what's ahead but use it to prepare my heart and mind for what You have in store.

Give me strength for today, courage for tomorrow, and faith for the journey ahead. Renew my spirit so I can walk gracefully, even when the path feels uncertain.

Lord, I surrender my plans, my fears, my dreams, and my burdens to You. Lead me, guide me, and align the steps that I will take with Your will. Let my waiting be filled with purpose, and may Your name be glorified through my obedience.

In Jesus' name, I pray.

Amen.

Patience in Practice

Patience is more than just waiting—it's an active process of trusting, learning, and growing. It challenges us to slow down, reflect, and align with God's timing, even when our timeline feels urgent. *"Patience in Practice"* offers thought-provoking questions to help you navigate seasons of waiting with grace and intentionality.

These questions are designed to shift your perspective, inviting you to explore what this season teaches you and how you can respond with faith and purpose. Let this tool guide you toward deeper self-awareness and a renewed sense of peace as you embrace the beauty of waiting well.

Understanding the Balance: The FLY Performance Curve

Before reflecting, it's important to understand how stress and patience interact. The *FLY Performance Curve* demonstrates that performance improves with a moderate amount of stress but diminishes when stress becomes too low or too high. Finding this optimal balance—your *"FLY Zone"*—is key to practicing patience effectively.

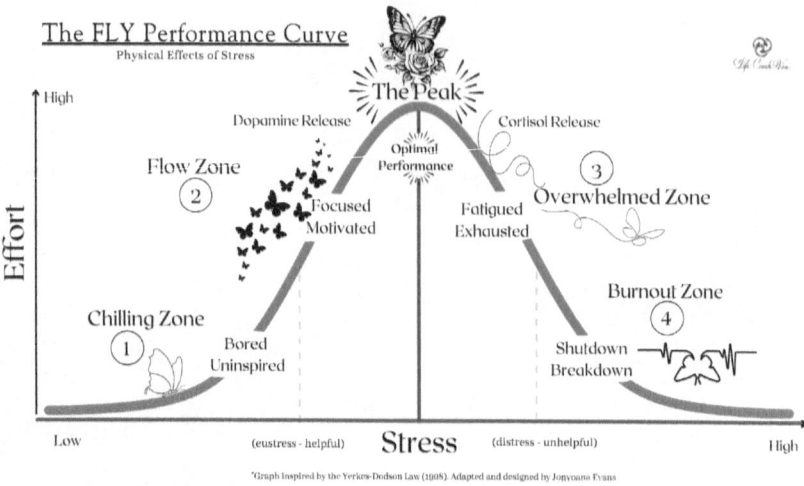

A diagram of stress and performance.

This graph illustrates how staying too far on either extreme of the curve—apathy or overwhelm—can hinder one's ability to wait well. Use it as a guide to assess where one currently falls on the spectrum of stress and effort.

- **Chilling Zone (1):** Feeling disengaged, bored, and unmotivated—this is the space of underload.

- **Flow Zone (2):** Gaining momentum, energized, and focused as you balance effort and stress.

- **The Peak/FLY Zone:** The optimal state where stress is managed, effort is focused, and you perform at your best. This is where growth, purpose, and patience align.

- **Overwhelmed Zone (3):** Stress starts to overtake effort, leaving you fatigued, distracted, and exhausted.

- **Burnout Zone (4):** Prolonged exposure to unhelpful stress leads to a physical, mental, and emotional shutdown.

The FLY Zone isn't just a stage on the curve—it's the ultimate target where you experience peace, productivity, and balance. Reflecting on where you are now can help you recalibrate, embrace patience, and work toward this space of growth and transformation.

Reflective Questions

1. **What stage am I in right now for this particular area? Egg, Caterpillar, Chrysalis, Emergence, or Adult Butterfly?** *(Reflect on what you've learned about each stage and how it applies to your current situation.)*

2. **Where do I fall on the FLY Performance Curve?** *(What steps can I take to move closer to my optimal performance zone?)*

3. **What am I learning about myself during this time of waiting?** *(Self-awareness can reveal strengths, weaknesses, and areas for growth.)*

4. **How is this waiting period shaping my character or faith?** *(Consider how patience, resilience, or trust in God is being developed.)*

5. **What small steps can I take right now to prepare for what I'm waiting for?** *(Focus on what is within your control while trusting God with the rest.)*

6. **Who has God placed in my life to support or guide me during this time?** *(Reflect on the relationships, mentors, or resources around you.)*

7. **Am I surrendering my plans to God, or am I holding on too tightly?** *(Evaluate whether you are trusting God's timing or trying to force your own.)*

8. **How has God shown His faithfulness in previous seasons of waiting?** *(Remembering His past faithfulness can help build confidence for the present.)*

9. **What would happen if I moved too soon? Am I ready for what I'm asking for?** *(Consider whether rushing ahead would be harmful or counterproductive.)*

10. **What specific prayers or scriptures can I lean on during this time?** *(Anchoring your waiting in God's Word and prayer can provide clarity and peace.)*

11. **What would this season look like if I fully embraced it instead of resisting it?** *(Shift the focus from frustration to acceptance and curiosity.)*

12. **What can I release that's causing unnecessary stress or distraction during this season?** *(Let go of things, thoughts, or habits that are draining*

your energy.)

13. **Am I confusing waiting with inaction? What can I do to stay engaged and purposeful?** *(Reframe waiting as a time for preparation, not passivity.)*

14. **What is God asking me to trust Him with right now?** *(Identify areas where you need to relinquish control and trust His plan.)*

Grounded in Gratitude

"**G**rounded in Gratitude" is more than a fleeting feeling—it's a powerful tool for mindfulness and transformation. Practicing gratitude shifts your focus from what you lack to what you have, cultivating a mindset that keeps you present and grounded. This intentional shift strengthens your ability to appreciate life's blessings and equips you with the patience to navigate challenging seasons. Let this resource guide you in focusing on what's working well, calming the urge to rush ahead, and trusting the process.

The Science Behind Gratitude Research has shown that gratitude has profound effects on mental and physical health. Studies reveal that people who regularly practice gratitude experience lower levels of stress and depression, improved sleep, and stronger relationships. Gratitude activates areas in the brain associated with emotional regulation and releases dopamine and serotonin, the "feel-good" chemicals. By practicing gratitude, you are literally rewiring your brain to focus on positivity and abundance.

The Spiritual Perspective From a spiritual standpoint, gratitude is an act of worship and acknowledgment of God's provision. Scripture calls us to give thanks in all circumstances, emphasizing that gratitude shifts our perspective and aligns us with God's will. *"Give thanks in all circumstances; for this is God's will for you in Christ Jesus"* (1 Thessalonians 5:18). Practicing gratitude draws us closer to God, reminds us of His faithfulness, and strengthens our trust in His plan, even during difficult times.

Practical Exercises for Gratitude

1. **Gratitude Journaling** Take five minutes each day to write down three things you're grateful for. They can be big or small—anything from a meaningful conversation to the comfort of your morning coffee. Reflect on why each item brings you joy or fulfillment. This practice helps you focus on the positive aspects of your life, even when challenges arise.

2. **Gratitude Walk** Go for a walk and use this time to focus on gratitude. With each step, think of something you're thankful for—your health, the beauty of nature, or the opportunities you've been given. Use this mindful movement to connect with your surroundings and recognize the abundance in your life.

3. **Gratitude Letter** Write a letter to someone who has positively impacted your life. It could be a mentor, friend, family member, or colleague. Share specific ways they have influenced or blessed you, and express your heartfelt thanks. You can choose to send the letter or keep it as a personal exercise to reflect on the power of connection and kindness.

Practicing gratitude is a simple yet profound way to realign your heart and mind with the goodness in your life. By focusing on what you have rather than what you're waiting for, gratitude cultivates patience, helping you trust that the right things will come at the right time. Whether through journaling, mindfulness, or acts of appreciation, let gratitude ground you, strengthen you, and propel you forward with a renewed sense of joy, peace, and purpose.

While They Waited: Lessons in Patience from the Bible

Waiting is hard. It stretches our faith, challenges our patience, and sometimes tests the foundation of our hope. Yet, waiting is also a universal experience—shared even by some of the greatest figures in the Bible. Each one faced seasons of uncertainty and struggle, but their stories remind us that God's promises are never late, and His timing is always perfect.

The Bible is filled with accounts of people who waited—not passively, but with trust, perseverance, and courage. Their journeys show us that waiting isn't just about holding on—it's about being transformed in the process. **"While They Waited"** shares ten stories that illustrate how patience and faith in seasons of waiting can lead to profound breakthroughs.

As you reflect on their journeys, I challenge you to dive into Scripture and read their stories for yourself. Let their struggles and triumphs speak to your heart and provide wisdom and hope for your own season of waiting. May their experiences inspire you to trust that God is working, even in the waiting.

1. David – Waiting to Become King

Theme: Preparation in Adversity When God anointed David king, he was just a shepherd boy. However, his journey to the throne was anything but immediate. For years, he lived as a fugitive, running from a jealous King Saul and hiding in caves. During this time, David learned to trust God's timing and developed the leadership skills he would need as king. His story reminds us that the waiting season is not wasted—it's preparation.

(1 Samuel 16-2 Samuel 5)

2. Joseph – Waiting for Leadership

Theme: Perseverance Through Trials Joseph dreamed of greatness, but his reality seemed far from it. Betrayed by his brothers, sold into slavery, falsely accused, and imprisoned, Joseph's path to leadership was riddled with setbacks. Yet, he remained faithful, and in God's timing, he was elevated to a position of power in Egypt, saving countless lives. His story teaches us that God uses even our trials to fulfill His purpose. *(Genesis 37-50)*

3. Ruth – Waiting for Redemption

Theme: Faithfulness and Loyalty Ruth's story is one of unwavering loyalty and faith. After the death of her husband, Ruth chose to stay with her mother-in-law, Naomi, and wait for God's provision. Through her faithfulness, she found redemption in Boaz, and her lineage became part of the story of Jesus. Ruth's journey shows us the power of staying true to God's calling even in uncertainty. *(Ruth 1-4)*

4. The Widow at Zarephath – Waiting for Provision

Theme: Trusting God to Provide The widow of Zarephath lived during a severe drought, with barely enough flour and oil to make a final meal for herself and her son. Yet, when Elijah asked her to prepare him bread first, she obeyed in faith, trusting that God would provide. Her small act of obedience unlocked a miraculous blessing—her jar of flour and jug of oil never ran dry, sustaining her household throughout the famine. Her story reminds us that trusting God can lead to abundant provision even in the face of scarcity. (1 Kings 17:7-16) reminds us that God's promises may take time, but they are never forgotten. *(Genesis 15-21)*

5. Hannah – Waiting for a Son

Theme: Prayer and Devotion Hannah's deep longing for a child led her to fervent prayer and unwavering faith. She poured out her heart to God, trusting Him completely. In time, God blessed her with Samuel, one of Israel's greatest prophets. Hannah's story encourages us to persist in prayer and trust God's perfect plan. *(1 Samuel 1-2)*

6. The Woman with the Issue of Blood – Waiting for Healing

Theme: Faith That Breaks BarriersFor twelve long years, this unnamed woman endured a condition that left her physically weak, socially isolated, and financially drained. She had spent all she had on doctors, but her condition only grew worse. Yet, in her waiting, her faith remained steadfast. When she heard about Jesus, she believed that simply touching the hem of His garment would heal her—and it did. Her story reminds us that waiting with faith can lead to miraculous breakthroughs, even when all hope seems lost. (Mark 5:25-34)

7. Moses – Waiting to Lead

Theme: Preparation for Purpose Before Moses led the Israelites out of Egypt, he spent 40 years in the wilderness, learning humility and reliance on God. His waiting prepared him for one of the greatest missions in biblical history. Moses' story reminds us that God uses seasons of waiting to prepare us for what's ahead. *(Exodus 2-4)*

8. Abraham – Waiting for a Nation

Theme: Walking by Faith Abraham was promised that he would be the father of many nations, but he waited 25 years for the birth of his son, Isaac. During this time, he learned to trust God's promises even when they seemed impossible. Abraham's story shows us the power of faith and obedience in the waiting. *(Genesis 12-21)*

9. The Prodigal Son's Father – Waiting for Restoration

Theme: Unwavering Hope for Reconciliation The father of the prodigal son waited patiently and lovingly for his wayward child to return home. Though the son squandered his inheritance and lived recklessly, the father never lost hope. When his son finally returned, repentant and broken, the father ran to meet him with open arms, restoring him fully into the family. This story reminds us that God is a God of restoration, and with patience, love, and forgiveness, broken relationships can be me nded. *(Luke 15:11-32)*

10. The Disciples in the Storm – Waiting for Peace

Theme: Trusting God's Presence in the Chaos As the disciples crossed the Sea of Galilee, a violent storm arose, threatening to capsize their boat. Filled with fear, they cried out to Jesus, who was asleep. When He awoke, He rebuked the wind and waves, and instantly, there was calm. Jesus then asked, "Why are you so afraid? Do you still have no faith?" Their story reminds us that even in the midst of chaos, God's presence brings peace. While waiting for calm in our lives, we are reminded to trust that God is in control, even when it feels like He's silent. *(Mark 4:35-41)*

Reflective Questions

- What similarities do you see between your waiting season and these biblical stories?

- How can you apply their lessons of trust and perseverance to your own journey?

- Which character's story resonates with you the most right now, and why?

Affirming the Cycle

Take a deep breath and allow yourself to pause. The journey through life's cycles can sometimes feel overwhelming, but affirmations can shift your mindset and anchor you in positivity. **"Affirming The Cycle"** is designed to help you navigate transformation—whether you're beginning anew, shedding what no longer serves you, embracing stillness, breaking through challenges, or soaring into purpose.

Affirmations are more than words—they are tools for realigning your thoughts, shifting your emotions, and visualizing the outcomes you desire. When spoken with intention and paired with hope and gratitude, they help you embody the changes you seek and face life's challenges with strength and clarity.

As you speak these affirmations, connect deeply with the emotions they bring and visualize yourself stepping into the truth of these declarations. Let them calm your spirit, inspire your actions, and anchor you in patience and purpose. Use them daily to guide your heart and mind, reminding yourself that growth is not linear but always intentional.

1. All that I need to survive and thrive already exists and is made available to me at the right time.

2. I release all anxieties that are associated with lack and trust that all my needs are met in abundance and in perfect timing.

3. I am the only one in this race; comparing myself to others serves me no purpose.

4. I am grateful for all I have and all that is coming to me.

5. Rejection redirects me toward elevation and purpose.

6. I understand that with every seed planted in fertile ground, there exists an even greater harvest.

7. Evolution is inevitable, and I embrace the change with confidence and excitement.

8. I release the need for perfection and celebrate the beauty of progress.

9. I am patient but persistent, remembering it's a process and celebrating the progress.

10. I am confident and deserving; I declare and decree abundance over my life.

11. It's the steps, not just the goals, that will get me there!

12. My goals' deadline has no correlation to God's designed timeline. I desire

His Will for my life.

13. It was not meant to destroy me, deter me, or define me; it was meant to develop me. For that, I'm grateful!

14. My mind is my greatest asset; therefore, I will accomplish the things I set my mind to.

15. My mind is peaceful and focused, yet inspired to create and grow.

16. Breathe in peace; release anxiety. I honor the present moment.

17. I accept the things I cannot change and embrace the courage to change the things I can.

18. I welcome positive images, thoughts, and energy into my mind and life.

19. I honor my body, mind, soul, and spirit as they carry me through this journey with strength and grace.

20. My heart is open to love, healing, and abundance as I embrace what God has for me.

The Butterfly Atrium Creed

I honor MY *commitment to my body, mind, and spirit.*

That **I will only** partake and extend that of *honesty, love, and true commitment.*

I understand that I ***have full control*** of what **I** *allow in it.*

I have *the power, the wisdom, and the foresight to dismiss **anything*** that does not align with it.

I will accomplish all that I put in front of me.

I beckon the support I desire to stand firmly beside me.

Doubt, fear, and obstacles are *way beneath me.*

My mind- **my greatest asset**, in which I *harness peace and clarity.*

We do *not* *back down at the first sign of adversity.*

This only inspires me, ignites me, and increases my propensity.

To pursue with no blinders or breaks on... ***it's my destiny***.

I possess some of the *same energy of the greatness that's above.*

I already have what it takes it's, even more, *stronger than love.*

I am created for *greatness*, nor you, nor you have to agree!

I am *confident,* **I am** *deserving,* **all of this and more** *is declared, and I decree.*

I honor my commitment to myself!

-Life Coach Von

"Maturity is measured by one's ability to embrace change and accept obstacles as opportunities for personal growth."

~ Dr. Robert L. Evans, III aka Dr. E.

(Ohhh, I loooove the way he thinks—that's my king!)

Waiting Well

Your Thoughts and Takeaways

www.ingramcontent.com/pod-product-compliance
Lightning Source LLC
Chambersburg PA
CBHW030907120626
46554CB00001B/40